COLOURED KEY TO THE
Wildfowl
of the World

by Peter Scott

WWT

D1344304

Wildfowl & Wetlands

A *Key to the Wildfowl of the World* containing black and white drawings only was first published in the 2nd Annual Report of the Severn Wildfowl Trust, 1948-49. It was reprinted as a separate book in 1950, revised and reprinted again in 1951. The first *Coloured Key*, with extensive additions and revisions was published in 1957.

Revised and reprinted 1961
Further revision 1965, 1968, 1972
Reprinted 1977
Further revisions 1988, 1998

Updated 2006

ISBN 0-900806-35-4

06 07 08 09

5 4 3 2 1

Cover: Red-breasted Goose by Peter Scott

Production by Paul Harding
Printed and bound in China by Printing Express Ltd.

FOREWORD

Wildfowl have a very particular charm. Their grace in the water, their perky deportment on land, the stunning variety of their colours during the breeding season, win them many devotees. No one during his lifetime did more to champion them than Sir Peter Scott. His paintings of them in wild and marshy landscapes captivated generation after generation of admirers – and still do. The ingenious techniques he devised to bring people and ducks – even wild ducks – close together, which he first developed at Slimbridge, led to the establishment of many similar reserves in Britain and countless others right around the world. And his scientific illustrations enabled anyone, anywhere, to identify any wildfowl he or she happened to encounter.

No single person was more responsible than Sir Peter for alerting the world to the urgent and vital need for nature conservation. Throughout his life he laboured tirelessly to protect animals and plants of all kinds. Even so, I suspect that had he been forced to pick one group of animals of which he was specially fond, it would have been the birds to which this book is such a vivid and lovely guide. It was first published some 50 years ago and it is good to see that after being updated scientifically it is being republished to aid and delight another generation. But that is not surprising – for I do not see how it could be bettered.

Sir David Attenborough, O.M., C.H., C.V.O., C.B.E., F.R.S.

COLOURED KEY TO THE
Wildfowl
of the World

by Peter Scott

Although many species and subspecies of wildfowl remain endangered or very scarce, there have been no further extinctions since the disappearance of the Madagascar White-eye (Plate 17) in 1991.

The taxonomy of the wildfowl family continues to be subject to scrutiny and a number of changes have been incorporated in this edition, as explained on page 32 and in the text facing several of the plates. With the publication in 2005 of the major two-volume 'Ducks, Geese and Swans', edited by Janet Kear, and published by Oxford University Press in their 'Bird Families' series, it has been decided to follow the classification and the names of the birds (both vernacular and scientific) used in that work. Interested readers will find comprehensive species accounts and much more detailed information on distribution, illustrated with maps, in the two volumes.

CONTENTS

ACKNOWLEDGEMENT

In this 11th revised edition, I would like first of all to thank Barbara Cooper who has been mainly responsible for getting this edition off the ground. She has given much of her precious time to organising all the processes involved.

I would also like to thank Malcolm Ogilvie for further up-dating the text and David Salmon for the revised information on the Wildfowl and Wetlands Trust. Hugh Boyd, who originally helped to compile the introduction, key and index should not be forgotten and is thanked again for his contribution.

Philippa Scott

Lady Scott

INTRODUCTION

In this Key there is a coloured picture of every kind of duck, goose or swan so far known to exist in the world – 245 kinds. The object of the book is to enable anyone, even without previous experience, to identify any bird within this group (called the family Anatidae) which they may see, and to discover its geographical range. It assumes that the bird has been seen at reasonably close quarters on the ground or on the water. The illustrations mainly show the birds in full breeding plumage. From June until October the drakes of many of the species of ducks from the Northern Hemisphere go into a dull 'eclipse plumage', which includes the period when the flight feathers are moulted and the birds are flightless. In this eclipse plumage the male in most cases looks very much like the female. The appearance of the females shows no striking change during the year, although it is sometimes affected by wear and tear of the feathers.

Where only one bird is shown as representative of each kind, as in the swans, geese, whistling ducks, etc., the sexes are virtually the same in plumage or, as in certain species of ducks, very similar but with the females slightly duller. In a few cases the female is so similar to that of a closely allied race that she is omitted in order to save space.

In the Key that follows and against the birds in the plates the conventional signs have been used to indicate sex, thus:

♂ = male   ♀ = female
♂♂ = males   ♀♀ = females

HOW TO USE THIS KEY

Each plate shows a group of species which are regarded as being particularly closely related so that in general the birds most likely to be confused with one another are shown on the same page. As a quick guide a certain number of basic characters such as size, shape, colour, behaviour and voice may give a clue to the page you want.

See, first of all, whether you can allocate the bird you are trying to identify to one or more of the headings on the following pages, and then see if you can trace it to a particular plate. Once you have the right plate there should be no great difficulty in making a final identification.

Relative sizes

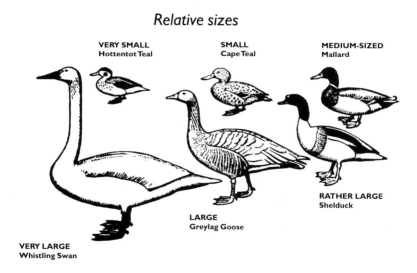

VERY SMALL
Hottentot Teal

SMALL
Cape Teal

MEDIUM-SIZED
Mallard

RATHER LARGE
Shelduck

LARGE
Greylag Goose

VERY LARGE
Whistling Swan

1 Size

Very Large

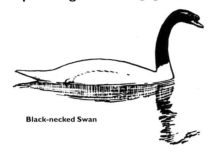

Black-necked Swan

Large

Muscovy Duck

Rather Large

Cuban Whistling Duck long legs, spotted flanks, rather dark 1

Shelducks and **Sheldgeese** long legs, upright stance 6, 7

Andean Crested Duck short legs, long body and tail, brown, with small crest at back of neck 8

Eiders thick-set, with massive bills, females brown, males black and white with light green on heads 15

Goosander ♂♂ long, thin red bill hooked at tip, largely white body, head black, dive often 22

Goosander ♀♀ long, thin reddish bill, grey body, brown head with crest at back, dive often 22

Musk Duck sooty-black, very broad, male with lobe hanging from bill 23

Eider

Very Small

Hottentot Teal black crown, cream cheeks with dark patch, bluish bill 9

Ringed Teal ♂ breast pink, flanks blue-grey, chestnut on sides of back 13

Brazilian Teal brown with coral red legs and feet, glossy green wings marked with black and white 18

Pygmy 'Geese' tiny goose-like bills, very short legs, backs black glossed with green 18

Bufflehead high crowned, largely white beneath, white patch on head, male cheeks glossed green and purple, dives often 21

**Cotton Teal or
Indian Pygmy Goose**

Small

Lesser Whistling Duck long legs, brown with
blue-grey sheen on back 1

Teals some males brightly-coloured, especially on
head, females brown 9, 10, 12, 18

Pink-eared Duck soft buff and brown, huge bill
with flaps at tip 13

Small Mallards, i.e., **Hawaiian Duck**, **Laysan Teal**
undistinguished 11

Smew thin pointed bills, male almost white, female
grey with brown head, dives often 22

Hooded Merganser thin pointed bill, male black
and white, female brownish, conspicuous flattened
crest, dives often 22

Stifftails very short and very wide, tail held flat in
water or cocked right up, dive often 23

Ruddy Duck

Medium

All the rest.

Pintail

2. Shape

Long Neck

Swans white, or white with black head and neck, or black, young grey or light brown 2

Magpie Goose black and white, legs orange-yellow, bill dirty yellowish, feet scarcely webbed 1

Spur-winged Goose black and white, legs flesh, bill dark red. 19

Pink-headed Duck probably extinct 13

Long Legs

Whistling Ducks noisy, sociable, addicted to perching on trees and posts 1

Hawaiian Goose brownish-grey with buff neck and black head, feet only partially webbed. 5

Orinoco Goose fawn and brown, dark wings, cherry-red legs, 'wind-swept' neck, very upright stance 6

Sheldgeese rather large, upright stance, small bills, most forms finely barred black on sides and breast 7

Cape Barren Goose large, grey, with green bill, pink legs and black feet, grunts like a pig 8

Spur-winged Goose very large, black and white, dark red bill and legs. 19

Elongated Body

Black-necked Swan very large, white with black head and neck, bright red knob on bill 2

Crested Ducks rather large, spotty brown, long black tail, inconspicuous crest at back of head 8

African Black Ducks medium-sized, dark brown, black backs with white spots 11

Hartlaub's, **Muscovy** and **White-winged Wood Ducks** large or rather large, short legs. 19

Sawbills long, thin bills, mostly black and white or brown and grey 22

Torrent Ducks pointed bills, upright stance, long tails 14

Short Rounded Body

Eiders rather large, females brown, males black and white with brightly-coloured heads and necks 15

Goldeneyes and **Bufflehead** medium-sized and very small, males, black and white females dark brown heads, dive often 21

Stifftails mostly rather small, with broad bills, spiky tails carried flat on water or cocked well up, dive often 23

Long Tail

Crested Ducks rather large, mottled brown 8

Pintails and **Salvadori's Duck** medium-sized or rather small 9

Torrent Ducks medium-sized, tail broad as well as long, upright stance 14

Long-tailed Duck ♂ medium-sized, black and white 21

Stifftails mostly rather small, dive often 23

Crest at Back of Head

Tufted Duck

Tufted Duck ♂ black and white, dives freely 17

Falcated Duck

Falcated Duck ♂ iridescent bronze head 10

Mandarin

Mandarin and **Carolina Ducks** males with larger crests, and very brightly coloured 18

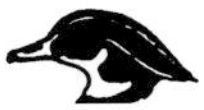

Carolina or Wood Duck

Crested Shelduck

Crested Shelduck rather large, long legs, probably extinct 6

Crested Duck

Crested Ducks rather large, long tail, mottled brown 8

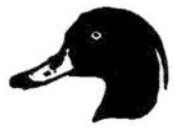

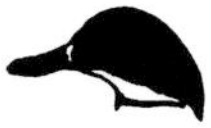

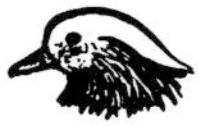

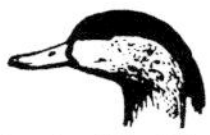

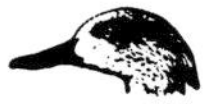

Marbled Teal small, beige-coloured with soft black
spots, crest inconspicuous 9

Marbled Teal

Mergansers long thin bills. 22

Red-breasted Merganser

Hooded Merganser

Goosander ♀♀ long thin bills, chestnut heads 22
Smew ♂ nearly white 22

Smew

Tuft on crown

Red-crested Pochard ♂ crown orange, like
shaving-brush 16

Red-crested Pochard

Cuban and **Spotted Whistling Ducks** long legs,
flanks spotted with white, tuft inconspicuous 1

3. Bill Shape

Long thin bill, hooked at tip

Goosander, **Merganser** and **Smew** (Sawbills) 22

Goosander ♀

Torrent Ducks bills bright red 14

Torrent Duck

Long, broad, spoon-shaped

Shovelers medium-sized 12

Shoveler

Long with flaps at tip

Pink-eared Duck small, light brownish-grey with
fine black bars 13

Pink-eared Duck

14

Making straight line with forehead

Swans very large 2

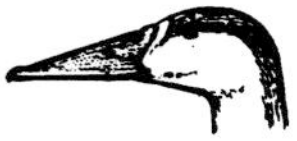
Swan Goose

Swan Goose large, with black bill and dark brown stripe down back of neck 3

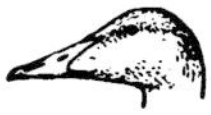
Eider

Eiders rather large, males black and white with coloured heads, females brown 15

Canvasback medium-sized – larger than **Pochard** or **Redhead,** dives often 16

Comb or knob above bill

Mute Swan very large, white, orange-pink bill, knob black. 2

Black-necked Swan white with black head and neck, knob red 2

Domestic Chinese Goose large, upright stance, imperious look, belly nearly touches ground 3

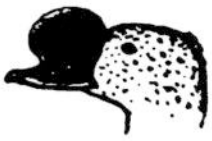
Comb Duck

Comb Duck or **Knob-nosed Goose** ♂ rather large, white head with black spots, knob black. 19

Muscovy Duck ♂ large, black glossed with green. Domestic forms white, grey or black, or mixtures, knob black or red. 19

Rosybill ♂ medium-sized, black and grey with cherry-red bill. 16

Some **Scoter** ♂♂ medium-sized, glossy black 20

White-headed Stifftail ♂ bill blue, dives often 23

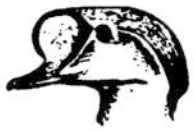
King Eider

King Eider ♂ medium-sized, black with pink breast, blue-grey head, knob orange. 15

Lobe hanging under bill

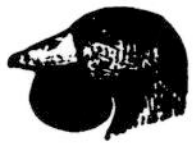
Musk Duck

Musk Duck ♂ rather large, sooty dark grey, dives often 23

Down-curved bill

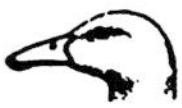
Blue Duck

Blue Duck medium-sized, grey, with flesh-coloured bill 13

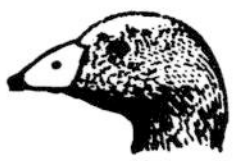
Cape Barren Goose

Cape Barren Goose large, grey, with greenish bill 8

Very large, heavy bill

Steamer Ducks large, grey marked with brown 8

Steamer Duck

Thick-billed Bean Goose large, brownish-grey,
orange band on bill and orange legs 3

**Thick-billed Bean
Goose**

Eastern Greylag Goose large, pale brownish-grey,
bill and legs pink 3

4. Colour

Very bright with complex pattern

Red-breasted Goose medium-sized, black, sharply
marked with chestnut and white 5

Baikal Teal ♂ small, with black, green, buff and
white on head 10

Mandarin Duck ♂ medium-sized, with orange
hackles and 'sails', white stripe on head 18

Carolina or **Wood Duck** ♂ medium-sized, with
glossy green and white head, purple breast, scarlet eye,
orange bill 18

African Pygmy Goose ♂ small, chestnut breast and
flanks, green patch on side of head, bright orange bill 18

King Eider ♂ medium-sized, black and white, with
pink breast, blue-grey and pale green patches on head,
orange-red bill 15

Steller's Eider ♂ small, black and white, chestnut
below shading to orange-pink, green patches on head 15

Harlequin Duck ♂ medium-sized, blue-grey and
white with chestnut flanks and sandy-orange stripe
over eye 21

White

Swans very large, long-necked 2

Snow Geese large, pink bill and legs, black wing-tips 4

Kelp Goose ♂ large, black bill and yellow legs,
all plumage pure white 7

Nearly white

Magellan or **Upland Geese** ♂♂ large, upright
stance, barred flanks, grey backs 7

Smew small, white, with some black markings on
head and back, thin, rather pointed bill 22

Immatures of **Swans**, **Snow Geese** and **Kelp Geese** 2, 4, 7

Black

Black Swan very large, long-necked, with white
wing-tips. 2

Muscovy Duck large, short-legged, black with green
or purple gloss, white patch on wing 19

Scoter ♂♂ medium-sized ducks, black with
coloured bill. 20

New Zealand Shelduck ♂ rather large, long-legged, with
green and white in wing 6

Sharply black-and-white

Black-necked Swan very large, white, with
black neck. 2

Magpie Goose large, white with black head,
neck and wings. 1

Common Shelduck rather large, white with black
head, neck and wings, chestnut band on breast, red bill 6

Goosander ♂♂ rather large, white with black head
and back, long hook-tipped bill. 22

Eider ♂♂ rather large, with white shoulders, white
or pink breast, black body, green patches on head 15

Tufted and **Ring-necked Duck** ♂♂ medium-sized
diving ducks with black heads, necks and bodies, white
or pale grey sides 17

Common and **Barrow's Goldeneye** ♂♂
medium-sized diving ducks with black heads,
white breasts, flanks and some white on the back,
white spot in front of eye 21

Chestnut

Ruddy Shelduck rather large, nearly uniformly
coloured, with paler head, black tail and wing-tips 6

Pink Head

Orange Head

5 Brightly-coloured Bills

Red Bill

Mandarin Duck ♂ medium-sized duck with orange
hackles and 'sails', white stripe on head 18

Red Spot on Bill

Bahama Pintail warm brown with dark crown and
white cheeks, bill blue with red spot at base 9

Indian and **Burma Spotbills** pale mallards with
white in wing, yellow tip to bill and red spot at base 11

Orange Bill

Pacific, **Northern** or **King Eider** ♂♂
rather large black and white duck. 15

White-winged Wood Duck rather large,
blackish-brown with spotty white head and spotty bill. 19

African Pygmy Goose small duck, dark green
above and chestnut on breast and flanks. 18

Western Greylag Goose large brownish-grey bird
with pinkish legs 3

Bean Geese large brownish-grey birds with orange
legs and some black on bill. 3

Carolina or **Wood Duck** ♂ medium-sized duck
with glossy green and white head, purple breast,
scarlet eye 18

Yellow Bill

Magpie Goose large black and white, bill variously
covered with dark scaly spots 1

Bar-headed Goose large pale grey goose with black
bars over head. 4

Spectacled Eider ♂ rather large black and white
duck with pale green on head 15

Greenland Whitefront rather large dark brown
goose with white forehead and orange legs 3

Abyssinian and **African Yellowbills** medium-sized
dark brown mottled ducks with black stripe down
centre of bright yellow bill 11

Green Bill

Cape Barren Goose large grey goose with green
top to bill 8

Blue Bill

Red-breasted Goose

6. Voice

Trumpeting or bugling

Honking

Whistling

Barking

Quacking

Dabbling Duck ♀♀ medium-sized or small,
mainly brown 9, 10, 11, 12

Clucking

Baikal Teal ♂ small, with bronze-green and buff
patterning on head 10

Shoveler ♂ small, with very large bill 12

Rattling or nattering

Radjah Shelduck ♀ medium-sized, white, with pale
pink bill and legs, reddish brown or dark brown on back 6

Crested Duck ♀ rather large mottled brown with
long tail and a small crest 8

Bronze-winged Duck ♀ medium-sized, brown
with white crescent on face and white patch under chin 9

Garganey ♂ small, white stripe above eye, brown
head, pale grey flanks, greyish back, sounds like
fishing reel 12

Blue-winged Teal ♂ small, mottled red-brown,
grey head with white crescent on side of face 12

Cinnamon Teal ♂ small, deep chestnut, with sky-
blue shoulders (usually hidden) 12

Smew ♂ small white bird with black markings
on head and back, thin sharp bill 22

Grunting

Cape Barren Goose ♀ large, grey, with green bill,
pink legs and black feet 8

Gadwall ♂ medium-sized grey and brown duck with
black under tail 12

Laughing

Common Shelduck ♀ rather large, black and
white, red bill, red-brown band across breast 6

Hissing

Mute Swan very large, white, orange and black bill 2

Egyptian Goose ♂ large grey bird with chestnut
brown markings, including patch round yellow eye 6

Muscovy Duck ♂ large black duck with black or
red lumpy bill, sounds like small steam engine 19

True Geese in defence 3, 4, 5

7. Behaviour

Frequent Diving

Male Goldeneye

Red-breasted Goose

Grazing

Perching on branches, posts, etc.

Red-billed
Whistling Duck

Mutual Preening

White-faced Whistling Ducks

IF YOU ARE STUCK

If you are unable to identify your bird from the Key or from the Plates the following possibilities should then be carefully considered.

The bird may be:

1 An immature specimen, the plumage of which is likely to be similar to the female, or intermediate between that of the male and female.

2 A male in eclipse plumage of one of the species in which the drake spends several months in a dull plumage usually resembling the female. Intermediate plumages occur during the transition.

3 A hybrid. These are comparatively frequent in wildfowl and the parentage is not always apparent even to an expert eye.

4 A variety or freak, showing white in patches (schizochromism) or a uniform paleness of plumage (leucism) or blackness (melanism). Pure albinism – pure white with pink eyes – has very rarely been recorded in wildfowl.

5 Descended from domestic stock. Such birds, capable of flight, include some tame grey or white or 'skewbald' geese (from Greylag stock) and Chinese Geese (Plate 3). Much more frequently mistaken for wild birds, however, are various forms of the Mallard (Plate 11) which show domestic blood and the domestic form of the Muscovy Duck (Plate 18), all of which may be quite good fliers.

Mallards showing domestic blood may take the following forms:

(i)   White Call Ducks (small; white with yellow or orange bill)

(ii) Cayuga Ducks (medium-sized; black or dark reddish-brown, with black head and variable-sized white patch on breast.)[1]

---

1 It has not yet been established whether these birds, which are not uncommon, are descended from domestic 'Cayuga' type stock or whether they represent a fairly frequent mutation capable of arising from perfectly wild stock.

(iii) Mallards with white wing-tips, broad white neck-rings, etc.

Muscovy Ducks with domestic blood can be:

(iv) Black glossed with green; white in wings; variable additional white, most often on head; bill swollen and bright red or black and red.

(v) Pure white with red bill.

(vi) Pale grey, usually with white head and red bill.

(vii) Mixtures of all three colours.

If you have seen a striking duck or goose which you cannot trace from this Key or from the Plates, it is very likely to be a Muscovy Duck, or a Mallard showing domestic blood, or a hybrid – in that order of probability.

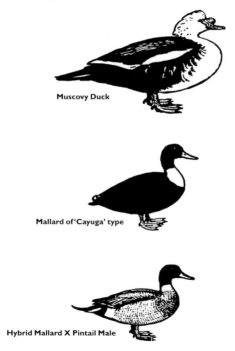

Muscovy Duck

Mallard of 'Cayuga' type

Hybrid Mallard X Pintail Male

NAMES AND CLASSIFICATION

All the birds in this book are given at least two names. Those printed in bold type are the English, or vernacular, names. The choice of these names is not governed by strict rules of procedure and people differ more or less strongly in their preferences. The ones used here are for the most part those in general use in ornithological hand-books. For species found in Britain these are the same as the 'common' names, used by wildfowlers and birdwatchers and those with just a general interest in the birds around them. But the text-book names given to species occurring elsewhere, in Australia for example, do not necessarily coincide with the names used locally. This Key tries to include the most widely-used of such local names, though confining itself to English ones.

The names printed in italic type are those applied to the different kinds of birds according to the formal procedure of taxonomy. It may be helpful to explain briefly the significance and use of such names. Taxonomy, the study of the principles of classification of animals (and plants), has two distinct components, classification and nomenclature. *Classification* deals with the ranking of various categories (such as family, genus, species) to which organisms are assigned in accordance with their evolutionary relationships, and *nomenclature* deals with the legalistic aspect of names (which name should properly be used for a given animal, according to the International Code of Zoological Nomenclature).

Classification has a double purpose. From a practical point of view, a system of grouping makes it easier to identify animals. From a theoretical point of view a 'natural' classification shows, to some extent, the relationships or supposed relationships of the groups con-cerned and helps to indicate the course which evolution has taken.

The system of classification applied to animals may best be demon-strated by means of examples taken from the text opposite Plate 1. The groups used are in a hierarchy, in which any category includes all the subsequent (lower) categories. The six universally recognised categories, in descending order of rank, are: Phylum, Class, Order, Family, Genus and Species. This system is expanded according to the needs of specialists in any group by using the prefixes 'super-' and 'sub-'. Birds belong to the Phylum *Chordata* (which includes all vertebrate animals and those animals without vertebrae which possess a notochord) and form the Class *Aves.* The swans, geese and ducks are included in the Order *Anseriformes,* one of twenty-three orders into which the Class *Aves* is divided. The Order *Anseriformes* includes the Family *Anhimidae* (the Screamers) and the family *Anatidae* (Swans, geese and ducks.)[1]

The Family *Anatidae* is divided into three Sub-Families. The Magpie Goose (Plate 1) is considered so different from all other wildfowl in the details of its anatomy that it is assigned to the Sub-Family *Anseranatinae* while the remainder are assigned to the Sub-Families *Anserinae* (Swans, Geese and Whistling Ducks) or *Anatinae* (the remaining ducks). Delacour and Mayr, whose paper *The Family Anatidae* (Wilson Bulletin Vol. 57, No. 1, pp. 3–55, 1945) provides the basis of the classification adopted in this Key, insert a further category, the Tribe, between the Sub-Family and the Genus. They use the term tribe (with the ending *-ini*) for a recognisable group of genera within each sub-family. The Magpie Goose forms a Tribe, a genus and a species by itself.

The Sub-Family *Anserinae* is divided by Delacour and Mayr into two tribes, *Anserini* – the Swans and Geese, and *Dendrocygnini* – the Whistling Ducks (Plate 1). All the members of the Tribe *Dendrocygnini* are assigned to a single Genus, *Dendrocygna.* But the Tribe *Anserini* includes four genera, *Coscoroba, Cygnus, Anser* and *Branta,* while the Sub-Family *Anatinae* is divided into seven tribes and includes 34 genera.

This lack of numerical equivalence between the groups shows the complexity of the relationships within the Family. But though it is difficult to give any precise meaning to the concepts, there is a general belief that genera and above all species form comparable natural units, whether in birds or mammals, or invertebrates or

---

1 Some consider that the Family Phoenicopteridae (the Flamingoes) should also be included in the order Anseriformes.

plants. The scientific name of Magpie Goose is made up of the generic name *Anseranas* (Goose-duck) and the species name *semi-palmata* (half-webbed). This use of the combination of generic and specific names to describe the most important recognisable natural group – the species – is the principle of binomial nomenclature, first consistently applied by the great Swedish taxonomist Linnaeus in the middle of the eighteenth century.

All these long Latin names are subject to a strict set of rules of nomenclature. Only the method of choosing the generic and specific names will be illustrated here, although rules are also laid down for applying the correct names to higher groups. The first principle of naming a species is that a type specimen of the organism shall be described under that name. The description must be detailed enough to make clear what differences are supposed to exist between the named specimens and other rather similar animals, and the species must be provided with a type locality, wherever possible the place at which the type specimen was collected. It has frequently happened that someone has described an animal as of a new species only for it to be shown later that a similar animal had been described earlier by someone else, so that two (or more) names are available for the same species. To get over this difficulty there is a rule of priority. The first specific name applied to a species must stand, except in very special circumstances, which have to be argued for any particular case.

The generic name consists of a single word, printed with an initial capital. The specific name is also a single word, written with a small initial letter. These, and all scientific names, must be words which are either Latin or latinized or are treated as such in case they are not of classic origin. The original describer can choose what specific name he likes, providing it agrees grammatically with the generic name. Usually the names chosen refer to a feature of the bird's appearance, or where it lives, though sometimes the describer names an animal in honour of a friend, or another specialist in the same group, or the collector who obtained the type specimen.

Three words in a scientific name indicate that the species seems to be made up of several more or less distinct groups, separated geographically, which though sufficiently alike to justify them being regarded as a single species, show sufficient variation from group to group to enable most individuals to be identifiable as members of one subspecies rather than another. (Subspecies are sometimes referred to as 'races' and as 'forms', and in this context the three terms are almost synonymous, though 'form' would also include species which are not subdivided into subspecies or races.) One of the subspecies repeats the specific name, while the remainder are given additional names. Some examples may make this clearer.

The Whistling Ducks of Plate 1 illustrate all these points. The Spotted Whistling Duck is called *Dendrocygna guttata*. *Dendrocygna* means 'tree-duck' – a reference to the long-necked appearance of all members of the genus, and to their habit of perching on trees – and *guttata* means spotted. *Dendrocygna eytonis* is named for the man who discovered and described the species. (It is not now usual for a taxonomist to name a species after himself.) Both these species show no signs of geographical variation. But the Wandering Whistling Duck *Dendrocygna arcuata* (the specific name *arcuata*, arched or bowed, refers to the flank feathers) forms three geographical races or subspecies. The Wandering Whistling Ducks of the East Indies form one subspecies. Since the type specimen of the species came from this area this subspecies must be called *Dendrocygna arcuata arcuata*. Australian specimens are larger and can be recognised as *Dendrocygna arcuata australis*, while specimens from New Britain, which are a good deal smaller, are distinguishable as *D.a. pygmaea*. (When generic and specific names need to be referred to repeatedly they can be contracted to their initial letters for brevity.) You will notice in the text that it is uncertain to which race birds from New Caledonia should be allotted. This kind of overlap is frequently found. Sometimes fuller investigation enables a clear-cut decision to be made, but often it must be accepted that such birds are truly intermediate, in which case, though the forms at each end of the varying population are given distinct names, the intermediate birds cannot be given a trinominal name and may be treated as *D.a. Australis ↔ pygmaea* or in some other inevitably clumsy way.

It will be noted that another name in Roman type follows the specific or subspecific name, e.g., *Dendrocygna guttata* Schlagel. This is the author's name. The author of a scientific name is the person who first publishes the name in connection with a description. The author's name is not always given as part of the scientific name, but is useful in making clear which type description is being used in cases where the history of the name is complicated. (There are uncomfortably many complications, because most names originate from 150 to 200 years ago, a period when first publications were often in obscure journals not widely circulated, so that species were often described as 'new' several times by different authors in the course of a few years.) Changing ideas about relationships have also caused the accepted limits of many species to vary. Changing ideas about relationships are responsible too for the presence or absence of parentheses enclosing the author's name. The rule is that the author's name appears without brackets if he originally described the species as a member of the genus in which it is now placed. But if the author placed it in another genus, then his name appears ijn brackets. For example, Eyton first described the Plumed Whistling Duck (in 1838) under the name *Leptotarsis eytoni*. Since it is now considered to belong to the genus *Dendrocygna*, *Leptotarsis eytoni* Eyton has been replaced by *Dendrocygna eytoni* (Eyton).

The contractions L. or (L.) which appear frequently instead of an author's name stand for Linneaus, the inaugurator of binomial nomenclature.

The 242 forms of swans, geese and ducks — all that are so far known to science — are comprised of 162 full species. Of these, 49 species, together with a further seven subspecies, have been found in the wild in Britain. These are marked in the text thus *. Two of these, Greylag Goose and Canada Goose, also have substantial free-living breeding populations stemming from released or escaped birds, as do the non-native Egyptian Goose, Mandarin Duck and North American Ruddy Duck. Several other wildfowl, both on the British

List and species which have never reached here in the wild state, have much smaller breeding populations that have arisen in the same manner. Five species and three races believed to have become altogether extinct throughout the world in recent years are marked thus †

The classification of the wildfowl has undergone a number of changes in recent years and these are reflected as far as practical in the text of this revised edition, though it should be noted that it has not been possible to alter the plates. The main changes involve the promotion of a number of former subspecies to full species status, hence the increase in the total number of species from 151 in the last edition to the present 162, and the consequent drop in the total of subspecies. These changes reflect both continuing traditional taxonomic work based on plumage and behaviour as well as recent advances using DNA in order to establish relationships. The latter technique continues apace and further changes are quite likely in the future. For example, the North American authorities have recently split the Canada Goose, with its 12 subspecies, into two species, each with a number of subspecies, and the British authorities are expected to follow suit. Neither the existing Canada Goose subspecies nor their ranges are currently very well defined and, given the amount of intergrading known to occur between several of the subspecies, the distributions set out on page 42, opposite Plate 5, should be regarded as very approximate.

SCALE OF THE PLATES

It should be noticed that five different scales have been used in the drawings – one for the swans (Plate 2), one for the True Geese and Sheldgeese (Plates 3, 4, 5, 7), one for the Shelducks and Perching Geese (Plates 6, 18), one for the Whistling Ducks, Crested and Steamer Ducks and Cape Barren Goose, and Scoters (Plates 1, 8, 20) and one for the rest of the ducks (Plates 9–17, 19, 21–23). This complication has arisen because, within the framework of the natural groupings, the birds have been drawn as large as possible in order to show the detail; teal would be too small to show the markings if drawn on the same scale as swans, all of which must be shown on one page.

Salvadori's Duck

TAXONOMIC CLASSIFICATION

Kingdom **Animalia**
Phylum **Chordata**
Class **Aves**
Order **Anseriformes**
Sub-order **Anseres**
Family **Anatidae**

PLATE I   MAGPIE GOOSE AND WHISTLING or TREE DUCKS

Sub-family   **Anseranatinae**
Tribe   **Anseranatini**

I   **Magpie Goose** *Anseranas semipalmata* (LATHAM) Southern New Guinea and northern and south-eastern Australia.

Sub-family   **Anserinae**
Tribe   **Dendocygnini**
(Whistling Ducks or Tree Ducks)

2   **Spotted Whistling Duck** *Dendrocygna guttata* SCHLEGEL Philippines (Mindanao). Indonesia (Sulawesi to New Guinea) and Papua New Guinea (including Bismarck Archipelago).

3   **Plumed** or **Eyton's Whistling Duck** *Dendrocygna eytoni* (EYTON) Australia, including Tasmania, but abundant only in the tropics; absent from south-west.

4   **East Indian Wandering Whistling Duck** *Dendrocygna arcuata arcuata* (HORSFIELD) Philippines and Indonesia (Borneo to the Moluccas).

5   **Australian Wandering Whistling Duck** *Dendrocygna arcuata australis* REICHENBACK Tropical Australia and southern New Guinea. Birds in northern New Guinea (and formerly in New Caledonia) probably belong to this form, or are intermediate between it and *pygmaea*.

6   **Lesser Wandering Whistling Duck** *Dendrocygna arcuata pygmaea* MAYR Northern New Guinea; formerly New Britain and Fiji, where it has probably been exterminated by the introduction of the mongoose.

7   **Fulvous Whistling Duck** *Dendrocygna bicolor* (VIEILLOT) South from southern California and Texas to central Mexico; northern tropical South America from Colombia to Guyana and French Guiana; West Indies; Brazil, Peru, south to Paraguay and northern Argentina; central and eastern Africa from Lake Chad to Natal; Madagascar; India, Sri Lanka and Myanmar (Burma), south to Pegu. (This is a most extraordinary distribution for any species of bird. There is no geographical variation throughout this huge and broken range.)

8   **West Indian** or **Black-billed Whistling Duck** *Dendrocygna arborea* (L.) West Indies (Bahama Islands, Greater Antilles – Cuba, Haiti, Jamaica, Puerto Rico – Virgin Islands, Leeward Islands, Martinique).

9   **Lesser** or **Indian Whistling Duck** *Dendrocygna javanica* (HORSFIELD) India from Sind eastwards to coast of southern China, south to Sri Lanka, Andamans and Nicobars, Malay Peninsular, Thailand, Cochin China, Riu Kiu Islands and Indonesia (south-western Borneo, Sumatra and Java).

10   **White-faced Whistling Duck** *Dendrocygna viduata* (L.) Tropical South America, south to the Argentine Chaco, Paraguay and Uruguay. Africa, south of the Sahara to southern Angolan and the Transvaal; Madagascar; Comoros Islands.

11   **Northern Red-billed** or **Black-bellied Whistling Duck** *Dendrocygna autumnalis fulgens* (L.) Extreme southern Texas and Mexico, south throughout Central America to Panama, where it may intergrade with *D.a. autumnalis*.

12   **Southern Red-billed** or **Black-bellied Whistling Duck** *Dendrocygna autumnalis autumnalis* SCLATER & SALVIN South America from eastern Panama to northern Argentina, but not south of Ecuador on the west side of the Andes.

The two races **11**
and **12** intergrade

Male has higher crown than
female

♂ and ♀ have the same plumage in
all the forms on this page

Medium

Small

Large

P.S.

PLATE 2   SWANS

Tribe   **Anserini**

1 **Coscoroba Swan** *Coscoroba coscoroba* (MOLINA) Breeds in southern Brazil, Uruguay, Paraguay, Argentina, Chile (including Tierra del Fuego), and, rarely, Falkland Islands. Winters further north, to about 25°S.

2 **Black Swan** *Cygnus atratus* (LATHAM) Throughout Australia (except north central) and Tasmania. Introduced into New Zealand in 1860s, and now widespread and common.

3 ***Mute Swan** *Cygnus olor* (GMELIN) Now breeds wild in British Isles, north west Europe, Russia, Caspian area and Iran, east through Turkestan to Mongolia. In winter to Black Sea, north-western India and Korea. Elsewhere widely introduced, e.g. North America, Australia, New Zealand.

4 **Black-necked Swan** *Cygnus melanocoryphus* (MOLINA) Breeds in South America, from 30°S in Brazil, Paraguay, Uruguay, Argentina, Falkland Islands and Chile, south to Tierra del Fuego. In winter north to Tropic of Capricorn.

5 **Whistling Swan** *Cygnus columbianus columbianus* (ORD) North America, breeding chiefly north of Arctic Circle from Alaska to Hudson Bay, and wintering on the Atlantic coast from Chesapeake Bay to Currituck Sound and on the Pacific coast from Vancouver Island to California.

6 ***Bewick's Swan** *Cygnus columbianus bewickii* YARRELL Breeds in northern Russia from the Kanin peninsula and northern Siberia, east to the Chuykota Sea. South in winter to Britain and Ireland and north-western Europe, the Caspian Sea, and Japan and China. Jankowski's Swan **(7)**, formerly regarded as a separate race on the basis of a larger, more yellow bill, is no longer considered as distinct from *C.c. bewickii*.

8 ***Whooper Swan** *Cygnus cygnus* (L.) Breeds from Iceland and northern Scandinavia eastwards to Kamchatka, Commander Islands and northern Japan. Winters in Britain and Ireland, western Europe, Asia Minor, northern India, central Asia, China and Japan. May formerly have bred in Greenland, where frequently seen.

9 **Trumpeter Swan** *Cygnus buccinator* RICHARDSON Formerly bred throughout North America. Now known to breed only in Alberta, British Columbia, Idaho, Montana, Wyoming and interior of Alaska. Population showing a welcome increase in recent years from perhaps only hundreds in 1930s to over 23,000 in 2000.

In the Swans the plumage of the
male and female (cob and pen)
is the same
Immatures are greyish with pale
flesh-coloured to orange bills

9

5

8

6

7

The two races **6**
and **7** intergrade

9

8

5

6

3

Adult and immature
The species which has become
largely domesticated

3

1

2

4

P.S.

PLATE 3   GREY GEESE

I   Swan Goose *Anser cygnoides* (L.)
Breeds in southern Siberia, Mongolia and
northern China from the Tobol and the Ob
to the Sea of Okhotsk and Sakhalin. Winters
in China. Domestic varieties of "Chinese Geese"
are derived from this species.

2   *Western Bean Goose *Anser fabalis fabalis*
(LATHAM) Breeds in wooded country of the Arctic
from Lapland eastwards to the Urals. Winters in
Britain (now very local), Netherlands, Europe
south to Mediterranean and Black Seas. Limits
of ranges of this and next four races not yet fully
determined.

3   Johansen's Bean Goose *Anser fabalis
johanseni* DELACOUR Breeds in forested western
Siberia east to Khatanga and south to about
61°N. Mingles and interbreeds with *rossicus* in
the north and intergrades with *fabalis* and
middendorfi where their ranges are in contact.
Winters in Iran, Turkestan and western China.

4   Middendorf's Bean Goose *Anser fabalis
middendorfi* SEVERTZOW Breeds in forests of eastern
Siberia from the Khatanga to the Kolyma, south
to the Altai. Winters in eastern China, Korea
and Japan.

5   *Russian Bean Goose *Anser fabalis rossicus*
BUTURLIN Breeds in Novaya Zemlya and on tundra
shores of Arctic Russia and Siberia west of the
Taimyr Peninsula. Winters in Europe west to
Belgium and Netherlands, south to Italy; in
southern Russia, Turkestan and China.
Individuals stray to Britain. "Sushkin's Goose"
appears to be a colour phase of this race, with
pink bill and legs.

6   Thick-billed Bean Goose *Anser fabalis
serrirostris* SWINHOE Breeds on the tundra shores
of Siberia, east of the Yenesei. Winters in China
and Japan.

7   *Pink-footed Goose *Anser brachyrhynchus*
BAILLON Breeds in east Greenland, Iceland and
Svalbard. Birds from Greenland and Iceland
winter in Scotland and England, those from
Svalbard in Denmark, Germany, Netherlands,
Belgium and occasionally France.

8   *European White-fronted Goose *Anser
albifrons albifrons* (SCOPOLI) Breeds on the Arctic
coasts of Europe and Asia, east from the Kanin
Peninsula, Kolguev and southern Novaya Zemlya
to the Kolyma River and perhaps beyond.
Winters in southern England, western Europe,
and on shores of Mediterranean, Black and
Caspian Seas.

9   Pacific White-fronted Goose *Anser albifrons
frontalis* BAIRD Breeds in Arctic America, from
Mackenzie River west to Bering Sea, and in
eastern Siberia, but western limits unknown.
Winters in western United States, south to
Mexico and east to Louisiana; and in China and
Japan. Now includes some populations formerly
considered as Tule Geese.

10   *Greenland White-fronted Goose
Anser albifrons flavirostris DALGETY AND SCOTT
Breeds in west Greenland. Winters in Ireland,
west Scotland and Wales; occasional in eastern
North America.

11   Interior White-fronted or **Tule Goose**
Anser albifrons gambelli HARTLAUB Breeds central
southern Alaska, within taiga zone, and winters
exclusively within Sacramento Valley of
California. Originally called Elgas's Goose,
A.a. elgasi.

12   *Lesser White-fronted Goose
Anser erythropus (L.) Fragmented breeding
range from northern Norway and Sweden
to north-east Siberia. Winters in south-eastern
Europe, Black and Caspian Seas, Turkestan
and eastern China. Rare straggler to Britain,
occurring almost annually in flocks of White-
fronted or Bean Geese. Population greatly
declined in last 50 years.

13   *Western Greylag Goose *Anser anser
anser* (L.) Breeds in north and west Scotland,
in relatively small numbers, with introduced
populations in southern Scotland and England.
Breeding range includes Iceland, Scandinavia
and northern Germany. Winters in Britain,
Netherlands, France, Spain and North Africa
(Morocco). Populations of central Europe are
intermediate between this and the Eastern race
and further study may reveal more distinguishable
populations. The Greylag is the ancestor of
domestic geese, other than Chinese.

14   Eastern Greylag Goose *Anser anser
rubrirostris* SWINHOE Breeds eastwards from
the eastern Baltic and central Europe (Austria,
Hungary), the Black Sea and Middle East
through central Asia to Kamchatka. In winter
to North Africa (Tunisia, Algeria) and the eastern
Mediterranean, Black and Caspian Seas, north-
west India and China.

The plumage of males and females is the same

Domestic Chinese Goose

1 Ancestor of the domestic form

The races of Bean Goose all intergrade

7

5

6

3

2

4

9

11

10

8 Adult

8 Immature

Black belly markings of adult Whitefronts vary individually within wide limits

Domestic Embden Goose Drawn to smaller scale

12

13 Ancestor of domestic farmyard geese; e.g. Toulouse, Embden, Roman, Sebastopol, etc.

14

P.S.

PLATE 4 SNOW GEESE, ETC. (ABERRANT GREY GEESE)

1 **Bar-headed Goose** *Anser indicus* LATHAM Breeds on lakes of high central Asia from the Tian-Shans to Ladakh and Kokonor. Winters India, Pakistan, northern Myanmar and China.

2 **Emperor Goose** *Anser canagicus* SEWASTIANOW Breeds on the north-west coast of Alaska from Kotzebue Sound to the Yukon and Kuskokwim Rivers, on St. Lawrence Island and in Siberia from the Anadyr along the Chukotsky Peninsula. Winters in the Aleutian Islands and the Alaska Peninsula, east to Bristol Bay; in Asia, south to the Commander Islands and Kamchatka.

3 ***Lesser Snow Goose** and **Blue Snow Goose** *Anser caerulescens caerulescens* (L.) Breeds on Baffin and Southampton Islands and Arctic coast of North America from Hudson's Bay westward and in north-eastern Siberia, probably as far west as the Lena. The Blue Snow Goose was formerly regarded as a distinct species but is now known to be a colour phase. It is most numerous at the eastern end of the range, but spreading westwards and becoming more numerous. Nearly all Blue Snow Geese winter on the coast of the Gulf of Mexico, chiefly in Louisiana. Birds of the white phase predominate in California, though some are found on the Gulf coast. In Asia, the race occurs south to Korea and China, but most of the Siberian population winters in the western U.S.A. Individuals of both types have occurred as stragglers in Britain, but most of those have been escapes from captivity.

4 ***Greater Snow Goose** *Anser caerulescens atlanticus* KENNARD Breeds on the coast of north-west Greenland. Ellesmere Land and the adjacent islands. migrates by way of Cap Tourmente at mouth of St.Lawrence to winter off Atlantic coast of U.S.A. from Chesapeke Bay to North Carolina, A straggler to Britain, though it is difficult to establish whether records refer to wild birds or to escapes from captivity in this country or elsewhere in Europe.

5 **Ross's Goose** *Anser rossii* CASSIN Breeds in the Canadian Arctic in the Perry River region, the west and north coasts of Hudson Bay and on Banks, Baffin and Southampton Islands. Winters in Sacramento and San Joaquin valleys in California and south to northern Mexico and the Gulf coast of the U.S.A. east to Louisiana. Has increased spectacularly from 2000 in 1949 to over 1 million in 2002.

2

5

This race has no
blue phase

4

3

White phase
Immature

3

Blue phase
Immature

3

Blue phase
Adult White-breasted form

3

Blue phase
Typical adult

3

White phase
Adult

These are two colour phases
of the same sub-species

4

3

5

I

The plumage of males and females is the same

P.S.

PLATE 5   BLACK GEESE

1 ***Atlantic Canada Goose** *Branta canadensis canadensis* (L.) Breeds in south-east Baffin Island, Newfoundland and Labrador. Winters on Atlantic coast from Nova Scotia south to Florida. Introduced into England in 17th century and now widespread. Also introduced elsewhere in Europe and in New Zealand.

2 **Central** or **Todd's Canada Goose** *Branta canadensis interior* TODD Breeds in northern Quebec, Ontario, Manitoba, around southern Hudson Bay and James Bay. Winters from southern Ontario, Wisconsin, Illinois and Chesapeke Bay, along Atlantic coast south to Florida and Louisiana.

3 **Great Basin** or **Moffitt's Canada Goose** *Branta canadensis moffitti* ALDRICH Breeds from central British Columbia, Alberta and Saskatchewan to north-eastern California, northern Utah, northern Colorado and South Dakota. In winter from southern British Columbia, north-western Wyoming and Arkansas, south to California and the Gulf of Mexico.

4 **Giant Canada Goose** *Branta canadensis maxima* DELACOUR Breeds western U.S.A. and south-west Canada, winters south-western U.S.A.

5 **Lesser Canada Goose** *Branta canadensis parvipes* (CASSIN) Breeds throughout the interior of northern North America from central Alaska east to Baffin and south to northern British Columbia and Manitoba, where it intergrades with *moffitti* and *interior*. Migrates mainly west of the Mississippi and winters in southern U.S.A. from California to Louisiana and south to Mexico.

6 **Taverner's Canada Goose** *Branta canadensis taverneri* DELACOUR Breeds in northwest interior from Alaska peninsula to the Perry River, where it intergrades with *parvipes*. Winters from Washington to Texas and Mexico, mainly in California.

7 **Dusky Canada Goose** *Branta vanadensis occidentalis* (BAIRD) Breeds around Prince William Sound and perhaps farther south along Gulf of Alaska. Winters within range and south to British Columbia and Oregon.

8 **Vancouver Canada Goose** *Branta canadensis fulva* DELACOUR Breeds along coast and on islands of British Columbia and southern Alaska. Largely non-migratory.

9 **Aleutian Canada Goose** *Branta canadensis leucopareia* (BRANDT) Breeds Aleutian Islands, winters California. Increasing due to protection in winter.

10 **Richardson's Canada Goose** *Branta canadensis hutchinsii* (RICHARDSON) Breeds on Melville Peninsula, Southampton, Baffin and Ellesmere Islands. Migrates between Mississippi and Rocky Mountains to winter in Texas and Mexico.

11 **Cackling Canada Goose** *Branta canadensis minima* RIDGWAY Breeds along western shores of Alaska. Winters from southern British Columbia to southern California, in large interior valleys.

12 **†Bering Canada Goose** *Branta canadensis asiatica* ALDRICH Extinct. Bred Bering Island (Commander Islands) and Kurile Islands, until about 1900.

13 **Hawaiian Goose** or **Ne-ne** *Branta sandvicensis* (VIGORS) Breeds on main island of Hawaii. Reintroduced on Maui and Kauai, where has bred. Probably less than 50 left in 1947. About 900 now alive in Hawaii, many more in captivity.

14 ***Barnacle Goose** *Branta leucopsis* (BECHSTEIN) Three discrete populations: breeds east Greenland, winters west Scotland and Ireland; breeds Svalbard, winters Solway Firth, Scotland; breeds Novaya Zemlya and west Siberian Islands and also islands in Baltic, winters Netherlands.

15 ***Russian** or **Dark-bellied Brent Goose** *Branta bernicla bernicla* (L.) Breeds in Arctic Europe and Asia from Kolguev east to Severnaya Zemla, mainly on Taimyr Peninsula. Winters on coasts of England and north-west Europe.

16 ***Atlantic** or **Light-bellied Brent Goose** *Branta bernicla hrota* (O. F. MOLLER) Breeds on coasts and islands of eastern Arctic Canada, northern Greenland, Svalbard, Franz Joseph Land. Winters in Ireland, Denmark and north-west England, and on Atlantic coast of U.S.A. from New Jersey to North Carolina.

17 **Lawrence's Brent Goose** *Branta bernicla orientalis* (LAWRENCE) Breeding area unknown, probably north-east of Hudson's Bay. Winters on coast of New Jersey. Very rare, possibly never existed as a distinct race.

18 ***Pacific Brent Goose** or **Black Brant** *Branta bernicla nigricans* TOUGARINOV Breeds on coasts and islands of western Arctic Canada, northern Alaska and Siberia, west to Taimyr Peninsula. Winters on shores of the Pacific south to Japan and northern China and from Vancouver Island to Lower California, principally in U.S.A. Occasional records of this race in Britain.

19 ***Red-breasted Goose** *Branta ruficollis* (PALLAS) Breeds on the Siberian tundra from the Ob to the Khatanga. Winters on western coast of Black Sea. Scarce in Europe, straggler in Britain.

12
Extinct

9
Apparent tendency
to white ring

11
Small and dark

10
Small and pale

6

5

4

7

8

3

2

1

17

18
Ring complete
in front

16

15

13

14

19

In all these forms the plumage of
both sexes is the same

P.S.

PLATE 6   SHELDUCKS AND SHELDGEESE

Sub-Family   **Anatinae**
Tribe   **Tadornini**

1 **Crested Shelduck** *Tadorna cristata* (KURODA)
Historical range in eastern Russia, southern Japan
and eastern China. Believed extinct in first half
of 20th century, but handful of records since seem
authentic. Likely area of survival on border of
North Korea and eastern China.

2 ***Ruddy Shelduck** *Tadorna ferruginea* (PALLAS)
Breeds in north Africa and from southeast
Europe, the Near East, the Caspian Sea, across
Asia to Transbaikalia, south to Himalayas and
south-western China. Winters in southern half
of its breeding range to the Nile Valley; India
and southern China. Occasional in Britain.

3 **South African** or **Cape Shelduck** *Tadorna
cana* (GMELIN) South Africa north to Namibia
and south-eastern Botswana.

4 **Australian Shelduck** *Tadorna tadornoides*
(JARDINE AND SELBY) Very numerous in southern
South Australia and Victoria and in Tasmania;
a straggler further north. Separate population in
Western Australia.

5 **Paradise** or **New Zealand Shelduck**
Tadorna variegata (GMELIN) Widespread in North,
South and Stewart Islands, New Zealand.

6 **Moluccan** or **Black-backed Radjah
Shelduck** *Tadorna radjah radjah* (LESSON)
Moluccas, Ceram, Buru, Waigiu. Salawati,
New Guinea and the Aru Islands.

7 **Australian** or **Red-backed Radjah
Shelduck** or **Burdekin Duck**
Tadorna radjah rufitergum HARTERT
Northern and eastern tropical Australia.

8 ***Common Shelduck** *Tadorna tadorna* (L.)
Breeds on coasts of western Europe, including
the British Isles; locally about the shores of the
Mediterranean, Black and Caspian Seas, east on
the saline lakes of central Asia to east Siberia,
Mongolia and Tibet. Winters from southern
part of its breeding range to northern Africa,
Arabia, India and southern China.

9 **Egyptian Goose** *Alopochen aegyptiacus* (L.)
Africa, south of the Sahara, also the Nile Valley.
Occasional records in Europe. Introduced into
England, Netherlands and Belgium.

10 **Orinoco Goose** *Neochen jubatus* (SPIX)
Basins of the Orinoco and the Amazon.

8

♀ ♂

1

Now extinct

♀ ♂

2

Slightly smaller

6

♂

♀ ♂

3

7

♂

♂ & ♀ the same
in both races

4

♀ ♂

10

5

♀

♂

♂ & ♀ plumage
the same

9

♂ & ♀ the same

There are two colour
phases, the second
being greyer on the
back than this one

P.S.

PLATE 7   SHELDGEESE

1 **Abyssinian Blue-winged Goose** *Cyanochen cyanopterus* (Ruppell) Highlands of Ethiopia.

2 **Andean Goose** *Chloephaga melanoptera* (Eyton) Western South America in the highlands of Peru, Bolivia, Chile and Argentina.

3 **Ashy-headed Goose** *Chloephaga poliocephala* Sclater Southern Chile and Argentina, Tierra del Fuego; Falkland Islands (rare). Migrates north in winter, but limits of breeding and winter ranges not clearly established.

4 **Ruddy-headed Goose** *Chloephaga rubidiceps* Sclater Falkland Islands and Tierra del Fuego; occasional in Patagonia and central Argentina. Northward movements in winter as far as Buenos Aires Province.

5 **Upland** or **Lesser Magellan Goose** *Chloephaga picta picta* (Gmelin) Chile and southern Argentina from the Rio Negro to Tierra del Fuego. In this form the males may be barred or white-breasted; the barred form predominates near the coast and to the south, the white form inland and to the north.

6 **Falkland Upland** or **Greater Magellan Goose** *Chloephaga picta leucoptera* (Gmelin) Falkland Islands. Introduced into South Georgia. Larger than the typical form and males are always white-breasted.

7 **Patagonian** or **Lesser Kelp Goose** *Chloephaga hybrida hybrida* (Molina) Coast of Chile from Chiloë, southward to Tierra del Fuego.

8 **Falkland** or **Greater Kelp Goose** *Chloephaga hybrida malvinarum* Phillips Falkland Islands.

All on this page except the
Abyssinian are South American

2

Male and female
plumage the same

I

Male and female
plumage the same

♂
White form

♀

6

♂

Males are never barred
in this form

♂
Barred form

♀

5

3

♂ and ♀
the same

4

♂ and ♀
the same

♀

7

♂

Local race
with longer
bill and legs

♀

♂

8

P.S.

PLATE 8

Aberrant species with affinities to tribe

Tadorni

1 Cereopsis or **Cape Barren Goose**
Cereopsis novae-hollandiae LATHAM
Two subspecies now recognised:
C.n. novae-hollandiae, occurring on islands off
south-east Australia, and *C.n. grisea* STORR, on the
Recherche Archipelago off Western Australia.
This species shows affinities with the swans,
especially the Coscoroba Swan.

2 Flying Steamer Duck *Tachyeres patachonicus*
(KING) Coasts, rivers, and interior lakes of
southern South America from Valdivia, Chile on
the west and Puerto Deseado, Argentina, on the
east, south to Tierra del Fuego; Falkland Islands.

3 Magellanic Flightless Steamer Duck
Tachyeres pteneres (FORSTER) The coast of
southern South America from Concepcion, Chile,
south to Tierra del Fuego, including the Straits
of Magellan to the eastern entrance, but not the
Atlantic coasts north of Cape San Diego.

4 Falkland Island Flightless Steamer Duck
Tachyeres brachypterus (LATHAM) Falkland Islands.

White-headed Flightless Steamer Duck
Tachyeres leucocephalus (HUMPHREY AND
THOMPSON) Chubut Province, southern Argentina.
This species (not illustrated) was first described
in 1981. It has more white on the head at all
times of the year than other steamer ducks.

5 Patagonian Crested Duck *Lophonetta*
specularioides specularioides (KING) From central
Chile and west central Argentina south to Tierra
del Fuego; Falkland Islands.

6 Andean Crested Duck *Lophonetta*
specularioides alticola MÉNÉGAUX Highland lakes
in the Andes from central Peru, south through
Bolivia to the latitude of Santiago, Chile.
Occasionally in winter to the central valley
of Chile.

Crested Ducks are probably more closely
related to the Anatini (Dabbling Ducks)
than to the Shelducks.

Larger, with buff chin

♀ ♂

6

Smaller, with white chin and mottled belly

♀ ♂

5

Magellanic Steamer is largest, coarsest, palest. Has less red on throat

♀ ♂

3

These Crested Ducks are probably more closely related to the Bronze-winged Ducks than to the Shelducks

♀ ♂

4

Flying Steamer is darker and smaller than the other two

♀ ♂

2

I

♂ and ♀ the same

P.S.

PLATE 9   DABBLING DUCKS

Tribe   **Anatini**

1 **Marbled Teal** *Marmaronetta (Anas) angustirostris*
(MÉNÉTRIÈS) Resident in Mediterranean Basin from
southern Spain to Near East, Iran, Baluchistan
and north-western India.

2 **Bronze-winged Duck** *Anas specularis* KING
Slopes of the Andes in Chile and Argentina from
the latitude of Concepción to Tierra del Fuego.
North in winter to the vicinity of Valparaiso, Chile.

3 **Salvadori's Duck** *Salvadorina
waigiuensis* (ROTHSCHILD AND HARTERT)
Mountains of New Guinea.

4 **Cape Teal** *Anas capensis* GMELIN
Africa from Botswana, African lakes, Uganda and
southern Ethiopia southward. Apparently not in
eastern coastal areas. Recorded from Lake Chad
and Senegambia..

5 **Hottentot Teal** *Anas hottentoa* EYTON
Africa from Angola, Uganda and Shoa to Cape
Province; Madagascar. Recently found in Chad.

6 **Northern Silver** or **Versicolor Teal**
Anas versicolor versicolor VIEILLOT South America
from central Chile, the Bolivian Chaco, Paraguay
and southern Brazil, south to central Argentina.

7 **Southern Silver** or **Versicolor Teal**
Anas versicolor frentsis KING Soth America from the
latitude of Valdivia, Chile, through southern Chile
and Argentina to Tierra del Fuego; Falkland Islands.

8 **Puna Teal** *Anas versicolor puna* TSCHUDI Puna
(highland plateau) of the Andes from central Peru,
south through Gbolivia (Lake Titicaca and
Cochabamba) to northern Chile.

9 **Red-billed Pintail** *Anas erythrorhyncha* GMELIN
South and East Africa from southern Angola,
Lakes Tanganyika and Victoria and southern
Ethiopia, south to the Cape; Madagascar.

10 **Lesser** or **Northern Bahama Pintail**
Anas bahamensis bahamensis L. Bahama Islands,
Greater Antilles (Cuba, Haiti, Jamaica, Puerto Rico)
northern Lesser Antilles, northern Colombia,
the Guianas and northern Brazil, as far as Amazon.

11 **Greater** or **Southern Bahama Pintail**
Anas bahamensis rubirostris VIEILLOT Southern Brazil,
Paraguay, Uruguay, south to northern and eastern
Argentina, and west to eastern Bolivia; central
provinces of Chile; recorded on west coast of Peru.

12 **Galapagos Pintail** *Anas bahamensis galapagensis*
RIDGWAY Galapagos Islands (Pacific Ocean west of
Ecuador).

13 **South Georgian Pintail** *Anas georgica georgica*
GMELIN Island of South Georgia (South Atlantic).

14 **Chilean** or **Brown Pintail** *Anas georgica
spinicauda* VIEILLOT South America from southern
Colombia and Ecuador, through Bolivia, southern
Brazil, Paraguay, Uruguay, Argentina and Chile
to Tierra del Fuego; Falkland Islands. Probably
does not winter in extreme south of its range.

15 **†Niceforo's Pintail** *Anas georgica niceforoi*
WETMORE AND BORRERO Eastern Andes of Colombia;
also Cali, Valle de Cauca, Colombia. Now extinct.

16 ***Northern Pintail** *Anas acuta* L. Breeds in the
northern parts of Europe, Asia and North America,
including British Isles. Winters south to West
Africa, the Nile Valley, Ethiopia, Persian Gulf,
India, Sri Lanka, Myanmar, Thailand, southern
China; from southern British Columbia, Mississippi
Valley and Chesapeake Bay to Panama and West
Indies; Hawaiian Islands.

17 **Kerguelen** or **Eaton's Pintail** *Anas eatoni*
(SHARPE) Kerguelen Island. Recently introduced
into St. Paul and Amsterdam Islands (all in
South Indian Ocean).

18 **Crozet Pintail** *Anas drygalski* REICHENOW
Crozet Islands (South Indian Ocean,
800 miles west of Kerguelen Island).

19 **Chilean Teal** *Anas flavirostris flavirostris*
VIEILLOT South America from central Chile,
north-western Argentina and extreme
southern Brazil, south to Tierra del Fuego;
Falkland Islands and South Georgia.

20 **Sharp-winged Teal** *Anas flavirostris oxyptera*
MEYER The Puna zone (highland plateau) of the
Andes from northern Peru, south through western
Bolivia to northern Chile and northern Argentina.

21 **Andean Teal** *Anas flavirostris andium*
(SCLATER AND SALVIN) High Andes of central
and southern Colombia and of Ecuador.

22 **Merida Teal** *Anas flavirostris altipetens* (CONOVER)
High Andes of western Venezuela and the eastern
Andes of Colombia, south to Bogota.

23 ***European Green-winged Teal** *Anas crecca
crecca* L. Breeds in Europe and Asia from Iceland
to China, Manchuria and Kurile Islands and Japan.
Winters as far south as North Africa, Nile Valley,
Somalia, Iran, India and Sri Lanka, Assam,
southern China and the Philippines.

24 **Aleutian Teal** *Anas crecca nimia* FRIEDMAN
Aleutian Islands.

25 ***American Green-winged Teal**
Anas carolinensis GMELIN Breeds in northern
North America from Alaska to Hudson Bay
south to about 40°N. Winters in southern
U.S.A., Mexico, northern Central America
and the West Indies. Vagrant to Britain.

Except where shown
these are all drakes.
The females are duller

6 and 7 intergrade
10 and 11 intergrade

Merida is a lighter version
of Andean
♀♀ of these 4 are almost
the same as ♂♂

P.S.

PLATE 10 DABBLING DUCKS

1 **Baikal** or **Formosa Teal** *Anas formosa*
GEORGI Breeds in Siberia east from the Yenisei
River to the Kolyma delta and Anadyr, south
to Lake Baikal, northern Sakhalin and northern
Kamchatka. Winters in China and Japan.
Recorded from Taiwan, formerly Formosa,
but derives its name not from the island but
from the fact that "formosa" is the Latin
for "beautiful".

2 **Falcated Teal** *Anas falcata* GEORGI
Breeds in northern Asia, south of the Arctic
Circle from the Upper Yenesei to Kamchatka,
south to Lake Baikal, northern Mongolia, the
Amur and Ussuriland. Winters in Japan, Korea,
eastern and southern China to Myanmar.

3 **Madagascar Teal** *Anas bernieri* (HARTLAUB)
Western part of Madagascar. Believed to be
very rare.

4 **Indonesian Grey Teal** *Anas gibberifrons*
S. MULLER Central Indonesia – Java, Celebes,
Lesser Sunda Islands, Sabeyer, Sumba, Flores,
Timor and Wetar).

5 [**Rennell Island Grey Teal** *Anas gibberifrons
remissa* RIPLEY Now extinct and probably never
a distinct race of Grey Teal *A. gracilis*.]

6 **Grey Teal** *Anas gracilis* BULLER Australia,
New Zealand, New Guinea, Aru and Kei Islands,
New Caledonia, Rennell Island. A recent arrival
in New Zealand, where it has spread rapidly.

7 **Andaman Teal** *Anas albogularis* (HUME)
Andaman Islands, Landfall and Great Coco
Islands (Indian Ocean). Two races have been
described from the islands, but since there is
striking individual variation in this species the
claim of *A.a. leucoparensis* not substantiated.

8 **Chestnut Teal** *Anas castanea* (EYTON)
Australia (except north coast); commonest
in Tasmania and southern Victoria.

9 **Auckland Island Teal** *Anas aucklandica*
G. P. GRAY Auckland Islands (400 miles south
of New Zealand). Lately reported to be holding
its own satisfactorily, though now extinct on
Auckland Island itself.

10 **Campbell Island Teal** *Anas nesiotis*
J. H. FLEMING Campbell Island (500 miles south
of New Zealand). Very rare, on Dent Island only.

11 **New Zealand Brown Teal** *Anas chlorotis*
G. R. GRAY New Zealand. Rare. Became extinct
Chatham Islands about 1915.

Erythristic form
of Grey Teal

High forehead

Smallest of the three

Island form of Grey Teal
with variable amount of
white on face

Dull plumage

Many males
are intermediate
between these two

Bright plumage

Narrower bill

P.S.

PLATE II   DABBLING DUCKS (MALLARDS)

1 ***Mallard** *Anas platyrhynchos platyrhynchos* L.
Breeds in Europe and Asia from Arctic Circle,
south to Mediterranean, Iran, Tibet, central
China, Korea and northern Japan; Iceland; the
Azores; northern and central North America,
west of Hudson's Bay and the Mississippi.
Winters from southern half of breeding range
to North Africa, Nile Valley, India, Myanmar,
southern China, Japan; southern Mexico and
Florida. Successfully introduced New Zealand,
Australia and South Africa.

2 **Greenland Mallard** *Anas platyrhynchos*
conboschas C.L.BREHM Breeds on coasts of
Greenland, on the west, north of Upernavik and
on the east, north to Angmagssalik.

3 **Florida Duck** *Anas fulvigula fulvigula* RIDGWAY
Resident southern Florida. Mottled Duck
A.f. maculosa once again regarded as separate
race, mainly resident Gulf coasts of U.S.A.
and Mexico.

4 **Mexican Duck** *Anas diazi* (RIDGWAY) Highlands
of central Mexico and the upper Rio Grande
Valley from El Paso, Texas to Albuquerque,
New Mexico.

5 ***North American Black Duck**
Anas rubripes BREWSTER Breeds in north-eastern
North America from the west side of Hudson
Bay to Labrador, and south to North Carolina.
Winters south to the Gulf coast. Recorded very
rarely in British Isles.

6 **Haweaiian Duck** *Anas wyvilliana* SCLATER
Resident Kauai, reintroduced Oahu and Hawaii
islands. Population has increased to c.2500
(1993).

7 **Laysan Teal** *Anas laysanensis* ROTHSCHILD
Laysan Island (900 miles west of Honolulu).
Once very scarce (only 7 individuals left in 1912)
but has increased substantially and in 2001
numbered about 450.

8 **Indian Spotbill** *Ansa poecilorhyncha*
poecilorhyncha FORSTER India to western Assam;
Sri Lanka.

9 **Burmese Spotbill** *Anas poecilorhyncha*
haringtoni (OATES) Myanmar, Shan States,
Yunnan (south China), also Vietnam, Laos
and Cambodia.

10 **Chinese Spotbill** *Anas poecilorhyncha*
zonoryncha SWINHOE Breeds in eastern Siberia,
Manchuria, Mongolia, northern China, Korea,
southern Sakhalin, the Kurikle Islands and Japan.
Winters south to southern China and Taiwan.

11 **New Zealand Grey Duck** *Anas superciliosa*
superciliosa GMELIN New Zealand and
neighbouring islands.

12 **Pelew Island Grey Duck** *Anas superciliosa*
pelewensis HARTLAUB AND FINISCH Pelew Islands
(east of Philippine Islands), northern New
Guinea, Solomon Islands, Fiji, Samona, Tonga,
Tahiti, New Caledonia, New Hebrides, Bismarck
Archipelago.

13 **Australian Black Duck** *Anas superciliosa*
rogersi MATHEWS Australia and Tasmania,
and much of Indonesia.

DNA studies suggest that the division of the
Grey Duck *Anas superciliosa* into three subspecies
is probably not justified.

14 **Philippine Duck** *Anas luzonica* FRASER
Philippine Islands.

15 **Meller's Duck** *Anas melleri* SCLATER Eastern half
of Madagascar; introduced into Mauritius.

16 **African Yellowbill** *Amnas undulata undulata*
DU BOIS Africa from Angola, Uganda and Kenya
southward.

17 **Abyssinian Yellowbill** *Anas undulata ruppeli*
BLYTH Upper Blue Nile and Ethiopian Lake
Region. Probably also Cameroon (one collected).

18 **African Black Duck** *Anas sparsa sparsa* EYTON
South Africa; northern limits of range not yet
known reliably, but as far as East Africa and
Malawi.

19 **Abyssinian Black Duck** *Anas sparsa*
leucostigma RUPPELL Ethiopia, Sudan, East Africa
across to the Upper Congo, and to Tanzania.
Rare in the western part of its range.

20 **Gabon Black Duck** *Anas sparsa maclatchyi*
BERLIOZ Western Equatorial Africa.
Probably not a valid race.

2

1 ♀

♂

Domestic Duck

Drawn to
smaller scale

5

4

3

Black spot

8

9

10

Bill deeper
yellow

Females mostly just
duller edition of male

12 ♂

13 ♂

♂

16 ♂

♂

Darker

Smallest

11

17

Largest

Greyer

14

20

19

These Black Ducks
intergrade

Female similar
to male

♂

18

7

6

15

Females also show
white round eye

Female like small
female Mallard

P.S.

PLATE 12 DABBLING DUCKS

1 ***Gadwall** *Anas strepera strepera* L.
Europe, Asia and western North America,
breeding from Iceland to Kamchatka and
Japan, British Columbia and Prairie Provinces
of Canada, south to England, Netherlands,
Germany, central Russia, Caspian, Siestan,
Transbaikalia, California and Colorado. Winters
south to northern Africa, Ethiopia, India, Assam,
southern China, Lower California, southern
Mexico and Florida.

2 **†Coues's Gadwall** *Anas strepera couesi*
(STREETS) Washington Is., New York Is. (Fanning
Group, 1,000 miles S. Of Hawaii). Extinct.

3 ***Eurasian Wigeon** *Anas penelope* L. Europe
and Asia, breeding in temperate regions north to
the Arctic Circle and beyond, from Iceland and
Scotland to Kamchatka. Winters in Britain and
south to Nile Valley, Ethiopia, India, southern
China and Japan. Regularly in small numbers
on the Atlantic coasts of North America, also
in British Columbia.

4 ***American Wigeon** *Anas americana* GMELIN
North America, breeding in the north from
Alaska to eastern Canada, commonest in the
west, and wintering from British Columbia to
California and the Gulf Coast, and from Long
Island, south to Costa Rica and West Indies.
Rare vagrant to Britain.

5 **Chiloe Wigeon** *Anas sibilatrix* POEPPIG Southern
South America from Chile and southern Brazil,
south to Tierra del Fuego; Falkland Islands.
Breeds in the southern half of its range.

6 ***Blue-winged Teal** *Anas discors* L. Formerly
thought to be separated into two races, Prairie
Blue-winged Teal *A.d. discors* **(6)** and Atlantic
Blue-winged Teal *A.d. orphana* **(7),** but now
considered to be just a single species. Breeds
Canada and U.S.A. from southern Alaska to
Newfoundland south to prairies, avoiding coasts
except in north-east U.S.A. Winters from
southern U.S.A., through Mexico, Central
America and West Indies, to South America,
south to Peru and Argentina. Occurs as a
vagrant in Britain.

8 **Argentine Cinnamon Teal** *Anas cyanoptera
cyanoptera* VIEILLOT Breeds in South America from
southern Peru, Brazil and Uruguay south, and in
Falkland Islands.

9 **Andean Cinnamon Teal** *Anas cyanoptera
orinomus* (OBERHOLSER) Puna region (highland
plateau) of the Andes in Peru, Bolivia and Chile.

10 **Borrero's Cinnamon Teal**
Anas cyanoptera borreroi SNYDER AND LUMSDEN
Breeds in highlands of Colombia. Exact limits
of range not yet known.

11 **Tropical Cinnamon Teal**
Anas cyanoptera tropica SNYDER AND LUMSDEN
Lowlands of Colombia.

12 **Northern Cinnamon Teal** *Anas cyanoptera
septentrionalium* SNYDER AND LUMSDEN Breeds in
western North America from southern British
Columbia to Mexico, east to Kansas and Texas.
Winters south to Colombia and Venezuela.

13 ***Garganey** *Anas querquedula* L. Breeds in
southern England, south Sweden, Finland,
Russia, east across Asia, south of lat. 60ºN to
Kamchatka; southern limits, France, Italy, Black
Sea, Turkestan, Manchuria and northern Japan.
Winters Africa south of the Sahara, south to
Zambia, Indo-China, Philippines, Celebes,
Moluccas and New Guinea. Regular in Australia.

14 **Argentine Red Shoveler** *Anas platalea*
VIEILLOT Southern South America from Peru and
Bolivia to southern Brazil and south to Tierra del
Fuego and Falkland Islands (rare); migratory in
northern and southern parts of its range.

15 **Cape or South African Shoveler** *Anas
smithi* (HARTERT) South Africa, north to Angola,
Botswana and the Transvaal.

16 **Australasian Shoveler** *Anas rhynchotis
rhynchotis* LATHAM Main strongholds in southeast
South Australia and south-west New South
Wales, and in Western Australia.

17 **New Zealand Shoveler**
Anas rhynchotis variegata (GOULD) New Zealand.
Formerly Chatham Islands.

18 ***Northern Shoveler** *Anas clypeata* L. Breeds
in Europe, Asia and North America, not north
of Arctic Circle nor in eastern Canada. Breeds
commonly in Britain. Winters as far south as
East Africa, Persian Gulf, Sri Lanka, Myanmar,
southern China, Japan, Hawaii, Lower California,
Mexico, Honduras, Florida and West Indies.

PLATE 13

Aberrant species with affinities to the tribe
Anatini

1 Ringed Teal *Calonetta leucophrys* VIEILLOT
South America from southern Bolivia, Paraguay,
south-western and southern Brazil to north-
eastern Argentina and Uruguay. The Ringed Teal
is probably more nearly related to the Cairinini
(Perching Ducks) than to the Anatini.

2 Blue or **Mountain Duck** *Hymenolaimus
malacorhynchos* (GMELIN) Confined to remote
mountain streams of New Zealand, mainly in
central North Island and the west of South
Island. Formerly more common and widespread.
Some authors have suggested the species consists
of two subspecies, on each main island, but this
is not yet generally accepted.

3 Pink-eared Duck *Malacorhynchus
membranaceus* (LATHAM) Australia, mainly inland.
Highly nomadic and varies greatly in abundance,
depending on rainfall.

4 Pink-headed Duck *Rhodonessa caryophyllacea*
(LATHAM) North-eastern and eastern India, Nepal
and Assam, south to Madras. Was always local
and rare, now almost certainly extinct. No reliable
reports of wild birds since 1935. Last in captivity
died about 1939. Probably a member of the
Aythyini (Pochards).

5 Freckled Duck *Stictonetta naevosa* (GOULD)
Occurs widely but erratically in Australia, range
changing in response to rainfall. Former threats
to survival from drainage and shooting now
greatly reduced.

This species seems to be more closely related to the Perching Ducks than to the Dabbling Ducks

♀

♂

1

♀

♂

4

Probably now extinct

Soft flap at tip of bill

♀

♂

Male's bill is only red in breeding season

5

3

In both these species ♂ and ♀ are similar

2

P.S.

PLATE 14 TORRENT DUCKS

Tribe **Merganettini**

1 **Chilean Torrent Duck** *Merganetta armata armata* GOULD Andes of Chile and adjoining parts of western Argentina, north to Province of Mendoza, south to Tierra del Fuego.

2 **Colombian Torrent Duck** *Merganetta armata colombiana* DES MURS Andes of Venezuela, Colombia, Ecuador and northern Peru.

3 **Peruvian Torrent Duck** *Merganetta armata leucogenis* (TSCHUDI) Andes of northern Chile, Bolivia and northern Argentina.

4 [**Turner's Torrent Duck** *Merganetta armata turneri* SCLATER AND SALVIN]

5 [**Garlepp's** or **Bolivian Torrent Duck** *Merganetta armata garleppi* BELEPSCH]

6 [**Berlepsch's** or **Argentine Torrent Duck** *Merganetta armata berlepschi* HARTERT]

Recent work indicates that the last three subspecies are no more than variants of *M.a. leucogenis.*

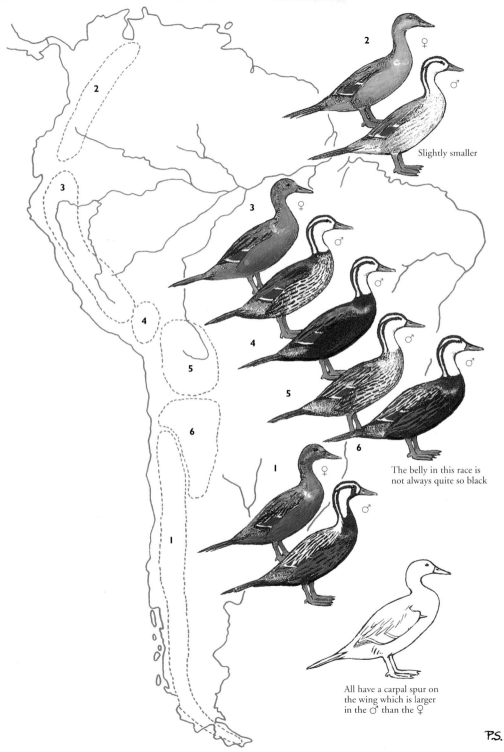

2 ♀
2 ♂

Slightly smaller

3 ♀
3 ♂

4 ♂

5 ♂

6 ♂

The belly in this race is
not always quite so black

1 ♀
1 ♂

All have a carpal spur on
the wing which is larger
in the ♂ than the ♀

P.S.

PLATE 15   EIDERS

Tribe   **Smaterini**

1   ***European Eider** *Somateria mollissima mollissima* (L.) Breeds in Iceland, Britain and Ireland (except Orkney and Shetland), Netherlands, Scandinavia, east to Novaya Zemlya. Mainly resident but some winter in North Sea and on west coast of France.

2   **Pacific Eider** *Somateria mollissima v-nigra* G. R. GRAY Breeds on Arctic coasts and islands of north-eastern Asia, Commander and Aleutian Islands and coasts of Alaska and Northwest Territories of Canada. Winters within range and short distances to south.

3   **Northern Eider** *Somateria mollissima borealis (C. L. Brehm)* Breeds on north-eastern coasts of Canada, Greenland, Iceland, Svalbard and Franz Josef Land. Winters in open waters within range and south to Maine.

   Hudson Bay Eider *Somateria mollissima sedentaria* SNYDER Resident in Hudson and James Bays (not illustrated).

4   **American Eider** *Somateria mollissima dresseri* SHARPE Breeds Labrador to Maine. Winters within and to south of range.

5   ***Faeroe Eider** *Somateria mollissima faeroeensis* C. L BREHM Faeroes, Shetland and Orkney; resident.

6   ***King Eider** *Somateria spectabilis* (L.) Breeds on fresh water near the Arctic coasts and on islands of Europe, Asia and North America. Rare straggler to the British Isles in winter.

7   **Spectacled** or **Fischer's Eider** *Somateria fischeri* (BRANDT) Breeds on the New Siberian Islands and Arcutic coast of Siberia from the Yana River to Bering Strait and on the coast of Alaska. Probably winters in the Bering Sea north of the Aleutian Islands, but range uncertain.

8   ***Steller's Eider** *Polysticta stelleri* (PALLAS) Breeds on the Arctic coast of Siberia from the coast of Alaska. Winters on open waters of Kamchatka, Commander and Kurile Islands, Aleutian Islands and Kenai Peninsular (Alaska), and in Norwegian fjords and Baltic Sea. Rarely recorded in Britain.

The eiders are included in the tribe Mergini by some authorities.

2 Largest

3

♀

♀

Medium sized

First year drakes have
only patchy white
breast and back

♂

2

♂

Smallest

♀

5

♂

3

4 Medium

♀

4

♀

1

♂

Large

♂

5

♂

1

7

♀

♀

♂

6

♀

6

8

♀

7

♂

P.S.

PLATE 16 POCHARDS

Tribe   **Aythyini**

1 ***Red-crested Pochard** *Netta rufina* (PALLAS)
Eastern Europe and Asia, breeding from Spain,
southern France, Netherlands (few), through
lower Danube, southern Russia west across
Kirghiz Steppes to west Siberia. Winters
Mediterranean, India, Myanmar to China.
Scarce vagrant to Britain; small numbers
of escaped birds breed.

2 **Rosybill** *Netta peposaca* (VIEILLOT) Eastern
Bolivia and southern Brazil, Paraguay, Uruguay
and Argentina south to northern Patagonia;
central and southern Chile.

3 **South American Pochard** *Netta
erythrophthalma erythrophthalma* (WIED)
Western South America from north-western
Venezuela to southern Peru; eastern Brazil and
north-west Argentina.

4 **African Pochard** *Netta erythrophthalma
brunnea* (EYTON) Eastern Africa from Ethiopia
to Cape Province, and in Namibia and southern
Angola.

5 ***Canvasback** *Aythya valisineria* (WILSON) North
America, breeding in western Prairie Provinces of
Canada and west central U.S.A. north to Alaska.
Wintering south from California, Mississippi
valley, from New York to Florida, the Gulf States
and Mexico. Vagrant to Britain.

6 ***European Pochard** *Aythya ferina* (L.)
Breeds in Britain and Ireland, southern
Scandinavia and central Russia through west
Siberia to Lake Baikal, south to Netherlands,
Germany, Balkans, Black Sea, Kirghiz Steppes
and western China. Winters in breeding range
and south to West Africa, Nile Valley, India,
Myanmar, south China and Japan.

7 ***Redhead** *Aythya americana* (EYTON)
Breeds in western North America from Alaska
to Mexico. Winters in southern U.S.A., Mexico
and Central America. Vagrant to Britain.

2

1 ♀ ♂

2 ♀ ♂

3 ♀ ♂
Slightly smaller and darker

4 ♂
Larger, paler

Female similar to female South American Pochard

5 ♀ ♂

To distinguish these three, note shape of head, and, in the males, the colour of the back and of the eye

6 ♀ ♂

7 ♀ ♂
Round head

P.S.

PLATE 17 POCHARDS

1 †**Madagascar White-eye** *Aythya innotata* (SALVADORI) Northern and eastern Madagascar. Probably extinct; not seen since 1991.

2 ***Common White-eye** or **Ferruginous Duck** *Aythya nyroca* (GULDENSTADT) Breeds in southern Europe, Balkans, Poland and west Siberia to the Ob Valley, south to northern Africa, Iran, Turkestan, Kashmir, the Pamirs and southern Tibet. Winters in the Mediterranean, West and Central Africa, Nile Valley, Persian Gulf, India and Myanmar. Rare vagrant to Britain.

3 **Baer's Pochard** *Aythya baeri* (RADDE) Breeds eastern Russia and north-west China. Winters in China, Korea, Japan, upper Assam, Myanmar and Thailand.

4 **Australian White-eye** or **Hardhead** *Aythya australis* (EYTON) Australia, casual in New Guinea, New Caledonia, Indonesia and some other South Pacific islands. Has occurred in New Zealand.

5 [**Bank's Island White-eye** *Aythya australis extima* MAYR No longer considered a separate race.]

6 **New Zealand Scaup** or **Black Teal** *Aythya novae-seelandiae* (GMELIN) New Zealand, formerly on Chatham Islands.

7 ***Ring-necked Duck** *Aythya collaris* (DONOVAN) Breeds in central and north-western North America. Winters in southern U.S.A., south to Panama and West Indies. Accidental in Britain.

8 ***Tufted Duck** *Aythya fuligula* (L.) Breeds in Europe and Asia from Iceland and Britain and Ireland to the Commander Islands (Pacific), south to central Europe, Balkans, Kirghiz Steppes, Lake Baikal, the Amur and Sakhalin. Winters in southern half of breeding range and south to Nile Valley, Persian Gulf, India, south China and Philippines.

9 ***Lesser Scaup** *Aythya affinis* (EYTON) Breeds in north-central and north-western Canada and U.S. Winters in southern U.S., south to Panama and West Indies. Vagrant to Britain.

10 ***European Greater Scaup** *Aythya marila marila* (L.) Breeds in northern Europe and Asia, east to the Lena. Has bred Scotland. Winters on coasts of western Europe (including Britain), eastern Mediterranean, Black Sea, Persian Gulf, possibly east to north-western India.

11 **Pacific Greater Scaup** *Aythya marila mariloides* (VIGORS) Breeds in North America from Hudson's Bay to the Aleutians, Bering Island, Kamchatka and probably elsewhere on the eastern Asiatic mainland. Winters on Pacific and Atlantic coasts of North America, south to Lower California and the West Indies, also China, Korea and Japan.

2 ♀ ♂

3 ♀ ♂

5 Smaller, but perhaps not a separate race

1 ♀ ♂

Some females have white under tail, especially in autumn

4 ♀ ♂

7 ♀ ♂

8 ♀ ♂

6 ♀ ♂

9 ♀ ♂

Female in summer

10 ♀ ♀ ♂

11 ♀ ♂

Slightly smaller and darker on back

P.S.

PLATE 18 PERCHING DUCKS

Tribe **Cairinini**
(Wood Ducks or Perching Ducks and Geese)

1 **Lesser Brazilian Teal** *Amazonetta brasiliensis brasiliensis* (GMELIN) Eastern South America from the Orinoco, western Brazil, eastern Bolivia, Paraguay, Uruguay and northern Argentina. There is a light and dark colour phase of this race.

2 **Greater Brazilian** or **Schuyl's Teal** *Amazonetta brasiliensis ipecutiri* VIEILLOT Southern Brazil, Uruguay and central Argentina, south of Buenos Aires. The ranges of the races of *A. brasiliensis* are probably complicated by some migration.

3 **Australian Wood Duck** or **Maned Goose** *Chenonetta jubata* (LATHAM) Inland Australia.

4 **Mandarin Duck** *Aix galericulata* (L.) Eastern Asia from the Amur and Ussuri, south through Korea, eastern China, Japan to Taiwan. Introduced and now well established in England.

5 **North American Wood Duck** *Aix sponsa* (L.) Eastern half of the United States and southern Canada. Wintering in southern and south-eastern States. Also in the west from British Columbia to California (an entirely separate population).

6 **African Pygmy Goose** *Nettapus auritus* (BODDAERT) Africa from a line between Gambia and Kenya, south to eastern South Africa and Madagascar.

7 **Green Pygmy Goose** *Nettapus pulchellus* GOULD Southern Papua New Guinea, northern Australia.

8 **Indian Pygmy Goose** or **Cotton Teal** *Nettapus coromandelianus coromandelianus* (GMELIN) India, Sri Lanka, Myanmar, east to southern China, south to Malaysia, Indonesia and New Guinea.

9 **Australian Pygmy Goose** *Nettapus coromandelianus albipennis* GOULD North-eastern Australia, nowhere abundant.

Dark Phase

Light Phase

1 and 2 intergrade

How to distinguish the
females and eclipse
plumage males of

4

from

5

Although apparently closely
related no hybrid between
4 and 5 has been recorded,
probably due to chromo-
some differences

♂ with crest depressed

♂ with crest spread

Slightly larger
than Indian race

P.S.

PLATE 19 PERCHING DUCKS AND GEESE

1 **African Comb Duck** *Sarkidiornis melanotos* (PENNANT) Africa from Gambia and the Sudan, south to South Africa and Madagascar; India, Myanmar, Thailand, Cambodia and Laos.

2 **South American Comb Duck** *Sarkidiornis sylvicola* (IHERING AND IHERING) Tropical South America from Venezuela, south to southern Brazil, Paraguay and northern Argentina.

3 **Western Hartlaub's Duck** *(Pteronetta hartlaubi hartlaubi* (CASSIN) West and central Africa (Liberia eastwards; limits of range not known). Probably intergrades with *albifrons*.

4 **Eastern Hartlaub's Duck** *Pteronetta hartlaubi albifrons* (NEUMANN) African Lake Region and Congo westwards at least to Ituri River. Probably intergrades westward with *hartlaubi*.

These two subspecies are no longer separated as the colour difference on the head has been found not to be consistent across their ranges.

5 **White-winged Wood Duck** *Cairina scutulata* (S. MULLER) Resident Assam, Bangladesh, Myanmar, Thailand, Vietnam, Laos, Cambodia and Sumatra. Population in wild thought to number 800 (2002).

6 **Muscovy Duck** *Cairina moschata* (L.) Mexico, south through central America and South America to Peru on the west and to Uruguay in the east. The ancestor of the farmyard Muscovy Duck.

7 **Spur-winged Goose** *Plectopterus gambensis gambensis* (L.) Africa from Gambia to upper Nile, south to the Zambesi.

8 **Black Spur-winged Goose** *Plectopterus gambensis niger* P.L.SCLATER Africa, south of the Zambesi.

Domestic Muscovy, which
may be glossy green, grey or
white, or a mixture

In both races there is
a carpal spur, larger
in the male. It is nor-
mally hidden

The species from which
the farmyard Muscovy
was originally domesticated

♂ and ♀
the same

7 and 8 intergrade

P.S.

PLATE 20 SCOTERS

Tribe **Mergini**
(Scoters, Goldeneyes, Mergansers)

1 †**Labrador Duck** *Camptorhynchus labradorius* (GMELIN) Now extinct. Formerly bred in Labrador. Wintered south, probably to Chesapeake Bay, but chiefly off Long Island. Last one shot in 1878.

2 ***Common** or **Black Scoter** *Melanitta nigra nigra* (L.) Breeds in Iceland, Ireland, Scotland, northern Europe and Asia from Norway, east to the Taimyr Peninsula. Winters chiefly on coasts of western Europe (including Britain), and south to Mauretania.

3 ***American Black Scoter** *Melanitta nigra americana* (SWAINSON) Breeds in north-eastern Asia, Aleutian Islands, western Alaska, sporadically across northern North America to Newfoundland. Winters south to China and Japan, on the Pacific coast of North America from Alaska to Mexico and on the Atlantic coast from Nova Scotia to Georgia and North Carolina. Vagrant to Britain.

4 ***Surf Scoter** *Melanitta perspicillata* (L.) Breeds in northern Canada, west of Hudson's Bay in Quebec and Labrador, with a separate population in north-west Canada and Alaska. Winters from Nova Scotia to Georgia and from Alaska to Mexico. Occasional in Britain.

5 ***Velvet** or **European White-winged Scoter** *Melanitta fusca fusca* (L.) Breeds from Scandinavia and the Baltic, east to Yenisei. Winters on the coasts of western Europe (including Britain), the Mediterranean, Black and Caspian Seas, the latter probably from a small breeding population in that region.

6 **Asiatic White-winged Scoter** *Melanitta fusca stejnegeri* (RIDGWAY) Breeds in eastern Asia from the Altai to Anadyr, Kamchatka and the Commander Islands. Winters on Pacific coast south to China and Japan.

7 [**Pacific White-winged Scoter** *Melanitta fusca dixoni* (BROOKS) This subspecies is now included in *M.f. deglandi*.]

8 **American White-winged Scoter** *Melanitta fusca deglandi* (BONAPARTE) Breeds in western Alaska, north-western Canada from the Mackenzie to James Bay and south to North Dakota. Winters on the Pacific coast south to north Mexico and on the Atlantic coast south to the Carolinas.

Bills of drake
Scoters

Nail of bill more
curved in both sexes

♀

♂

♀

♂

3

2

Extinct

1

♀

♂

4

♀

♂

2

3

4

6

5

8

As above
but shorter

7

The females of all four races
of Velvet Scoter are almost
exactly alike

♂

♂

5

♀

♂

♂

7

8

6

P.S.

PLATE 21 HARLEQUINS, LONGTAIL AND GOLDENEYES

1 ***Harlequin Duck** *Histrionicus histrionicus* (L.)
Breeds Iceland, Greenland, northern Labrador,
southern Alaska, south in the mountains to
central California and Colorado, and in eastern
Siberia from the Lena and Lake Baikal to Anadyr,
Kamchatka, Sakhalin and the Kurile Islands.
Mainly resident, breeding on rivers and wintering
on sea coasts; some south to Long Island in
winter. Rare straggler to Britain.

2 [**Pacific** or **Western Harlequin Duck**
Histrionicus histrionicus pacificus W. S. BROOKS
This race always doubtfully valid and now
generally not recognised.]

3 ***Long-tailed Duck** or **Old Squaw** *Clangula
hyemalis* (L.) Breeds on Arctic coasts of Europe,
Asia and North America. Winters south to
Britain, Netherlands, France, Black Sea, Caspian
Sea, Japan, Alaska, the Great Lakes and North
Carolina, and in southern Greenland.

4 ***Barrow's Goldeneye** *Bucephala islandica*
(GMELIN) Breeds in Iceland, Labrador, Quebec
and in the mountains of north-western North
America from south-central Alaska to south-
western Colorado. The birds of Iceland are more
or less resident, repairing to the coast in winter.
Those in America winter along the St. Lawrence
River, and south to San Francisco on the Pacific
coast. Females in the Pacific population have
more extensive yellow on their bills. Vagrant to
Britain.

5 ***European Goldeneye** *Bucephala clangula
clangula* (L.) Breeds from Scotland and northern
Scandinavia east across Europe and Asia, north
to the limit of trees, south to Germany, Balkans,
central Russia and Siberia to Kamchatka and
Sakhalin. Winters from Britain and Ireland,
Mediterranean and northern India to southern
China and Japan.

6 **American Goldeneye** *Bucephala clangula
americana* (BONAPARTE) Breeds in North America
in heavy timber from Alaska and British
Columbia to Newfoundland. Winters on Pacific
coast to South Carolina. Also on open lakes and
rivers in central United States.

7 ***Bufflehead** *Bucephala albeola* (L.) Breeds
from central Alaska to Hudson's Bay, south to
British Columbia, Alberta and Manitoba.
Winters mainly in the south and west U.S.A.;
also Aleutian and Commander Islands.
Rare vagrant to Britain.

Darker chestnut streak

♂

1

Paler streak

2

White goes farther back

Heavier bill

♂

Slightly larger bird

2

♀

♂

Races doubtfully valid

1

♀

♂

The Longtail has two strikingly different plumages – summer and winter (and an eclipse in the drake in autumn)

3

♀

♂

Summer

♀

Winter

♂

♀ showing wholly yellow bill

♀

♂

4

6

Larger

♀

♂

♀

♂

5

Smaller

♀

♂

7

P.S.

PLATE 22   MERGANSERS OR SAWBILLS

1 ***Smew** *Mergus albellus* L. Breeds in Europe and Asia from Scandinavia to Siberia and south to the Volga, Turkestan and the Amur. Winters on coasts and lakes in Britain (regular on reservoirs near London), western Europe, Black and Caspian Seas, Iraq, Central China and Japan.

2 **Hooded Merganser** *Mergus cucullatus* L. North America, breeding from south central Canada to south-east U.S.A. and in British Columbia and Oregon, wintering chiefly in the Pacific states, Great Lakes, the Gulf states and the Atlantic states south of New York.

3 **Brazilian Merganser** *Mergus octosetaceus* VIEILLOT Southern Brazil, eastern Paraguay and north-eastern Argentina. Very rare and now probably extinct in Paraguay.

4 **†Auckland Islands Merganser** *Mergus australis* HOMBRON & JACQUINOT Found on Auckland Islands (250 miles south of New Zealand) from 1840 to 1902, but not since. Sub-fossil bones also found on east coast of South Island, New Zealand.

5 ***Red-breasted Merganser** *Mergus serrator* L. Breeds in suitable places throughout northern Europe (including northern Britain and Ireland), Asia, North America and Greenland, south in winter to the Mediterranean, Persian Gulf, China, Mexico, Gulf states and Florida.

6 [**Greenland Merganser** *Mergus serrator schioleri* SALOMONSEN This race no longer generally recognised.]

7 **Chinese** or **Scaly-sided Merganser** *Mergus squamatus* GOULD Breeds south-eastern Russia, north-western China (Manchuria) and North Korea. Winters in China from western Szechuan to central Fukien and south to western Yunnan, though full range unknown.

8 ***Goosander** or **Common Merganser** *Mergus merganser merganser* L. Breeds in Europe and Asia from Iceland, Britain, Scandinavia and the Balkans to Kamchatka, the Kurile and Commander Islands. South in winter to Mediterranean and Iran.

9 **Asiatic Goosander** *Mergus merganser comatus* SALVADORI Afghanistan, Turkestan, Altai, Tibet. Winters northern India, northern Myanmar and China (Szechuan).

10 **American Merganser** *Mergus merganser americanus* CASSIN North America, breeding south of a line from south-eastern Alaska to Newfoundland and wintering on Pacific and Atlantic coasts as well as across continental U.S.A.

2

♀

♂

1

♀

♂

6
Thicker bill

♀

♂

5

♀

♂

8

Greenland race no
longer recognised

5

10

♀

♂

♂

♀

Nail hooked

♂

9
Smaller

8

7

♀

♂

3

♂

♀ had single
white wing bar

♂ and ♀ similar

4
Extinct

P.S.

PLATE 23 STIFFTAILS

1 **Masked Duck** *Oxyura dominica* (L) Greater Antilles (Cuba, Haiti, Jamaica, Puerto Rico) and South America to central Chile and north-eastern Argentina. Small numbers occur on Gulf coasts of Mexico and Texas.

2 **White-headed Duck** *Oxyura leucocephala* (SCOPOLI) Breeds southern Spain and North Africa, where resident, and Turkey east through Kazahkstan to north-east China. Latter population winters from Turkey to Pakistan.

3 **North American Ruddy Duck** *Oxyura jamaicensis jamaicensis* (GMELIN) Breeds in north-west central North America and winters south to California, Mexico, Florida and the Carolinas; also resident in West Indies. Birds escaped from captivity have become established in Britain and western Europe, but are now being controlled because of threat to the White-headed Duck through hybridisation.

4 **Colombian Ruddy Duck** *Oxyura jamaicensis andina* LEHMANN Andean lakes of central and eastern Colombia. This race forms the link between *O.j.jamaicensis* and *O.j.ferruginea* and may intergrade in both directions.

5 **Peruvian Ruddy Duck** *Oxyura jamaicensis ferruginea* (EYTON) Breeds from southern Colombia down full length of Andes through Peru, eastern Bolivia, Chile and Argentina to Tierra del Fuego.

6 **Argentine Ruddy Duck** *Oxyura vittata* (R. A. PHILIPPI) Southern South America from central Chile, northern Argentina and Paraguay to Tierra del Fuego.

7 **Australian Blue-billed Duck** *Oxyura australis* (GOULD) In dense swamps in south-eastern and Western Australia.

8 **Maccoa Duck** *Oxyura maccoa* (EYTON) Two geographically distinct populations, in eastern and southern Africa.

9 **Musk Duck** *Biziua lobata* (SHAW) Southern Australia and Tasmania; in deep, permanent swamps.

10 **African White-backed Duck** *Thalassornis leuconotus leuconotus* EYTON Africa from eastern Cameroon and southern Ethiopia, south to the Cape.

11 **Madagascar White-backed Duck** *Thalassornis leuconotus insularis* RICHMOND Madagascar.

12 **Black-headed Duck** *Heteronetta atricapilla* (MERREM) Central Chile, east to Paraguay and southern Brazil, south in Argentina at least to the latitude of Buenos Aires.

Behavioural and anatomical work, confirmed by recent DNA studies, indicates that the genus *Thalassornis* is more closely related to the tribe *Dendrocygnini* than to the *Oxyurini*.

Two normal swimming positions

♂ displaying

Tail spread

3

Winter ♂

♀

Summer ♂

4

5 Broad bill

♀

♂

1 ♀

♂

These three races intergrade, the white cheeks (not always present in **4**) are progressively lost

6 ♀

Narrow bill

♂

8 ♀

♂

♀

♂

7

10 ♂ and ♀ the same

11

Normal swimming position

Smaller and brighter

♂ and ♀ the same

12

Parasitic, laying in other bird's nests

♀

♂

9

P.S.

INDEX OF SCIENTIFIC NAMES

Figures opposite names refer to plate numbers. Names of genera are shown in **bold**, of species and subspecies in roman type. Where a species includes several subspecies the subspecific name only is cited with that of the genus: e.g., *Dendrocygna arcuata arcuata* is listed as 'arcuata, Dendrocygna' while *Dendrocygna arcuata australis* appears as 'australis, Dendrocygna'. The names of genera and species shown in parenthesis are synonyms no longer in use. Only names which have been widely used, but are now discarded, are included in the synonymy.

INDEX OF ENGLISH NAMES

The application of English names to birds is not governed by formal procedure such as governs the scientific terminology. This index is correspondingly unsystematic. It aims at enabling the reader to find the illustrations of every species, and so it includes a number of names in local or general use even though alternative names have been employed in the text. Such additional names are shown in italic type, followed immediately by the preferred name, in roman type.

Although it seemed desirable to provide in the text a distinctive English name for every subspecies, these lengthy names are rarely used, the specific name being the obvious choice. Accordingly in this index only the specific vernacular names are given except in those cases where one subspecies has acquired a distinctive English name of its own. For example, twelve races of Canada Goose are illustrated on plate 5: in this index all are covered by the entry 'Canada Goose', but 'Cackling Goose' is also included, because this bird is not generally known as the 'Cackling Canada Goose'.

A few names not originally English have also been included, e.g., 'Ne-ne' for the Hawaiian Goose, familiarity being the criterion.

THE WILDFOWL
AND WETLANDS TRUST

Sir Peter Scott founded the Wildfowl & Wetlands Trust (WWT) at Slimbridge in 1946. His aim was 'to establish a centre for the scientific study, public display and conservation of the wildfowl of the world'.

WWT is the UK's only specialist wetland conservation charity with a national network of wetland visitor centres. It is a world leader for the protection of swans, geese, ducks and flamingos.

Two derelict cottages near the small Gloucestershire village of Slimbridge on the Severn Estuary formed WWT's first headquarters, with four wartime defence pill-boxes acting as hides from which to observe wild birds. From these early beginnings, the organisation has grown into one with nine centres and over 130,000 members, employing some 300 staff and managing over 1,600 hectares of wetland habitat (including six Sites of Special Scientific Interest and five Ramsar sites).

Wetlands are the places where land and water meet and stretch to the open water beyond - ponds, lakes, rivers, marshes, swamps, estuaries and seashores. In the UK alone, half of our wetlands have been lost in the last century, and all over the globe the loss of all wetlands is accelerating as populations and pressure for resources soar.

The survival of many of the world's swans, geese, ducks, flamingos and other waterbirds living in wetlands is threatened, while many other wetland wildlife species lose their homes every time a wetland is destroyed or damaged.

WWT works throughout the UK and worldwide to:
- Save and restore ponds, lakes, rivers, marshes and other wetlands
- Save threatened ducks, geese, swans, flamingos and other waterbirds
- Protect wetland wildlife and plants
- Enrich people's lives, through learning about and being close to nature.

WWT Centres

WWT's nine centres are all different, but all are designed to meet the needs of both visitors and wildlife. The sites were chosen for their potential value to wildlife, and developed to share this wildlife with people. Visit a WWT centre at any time of year and you will be guaranteed a different experience each time. The landscape constantly changes: the colourful yellow, red and purple hues of wetland flowers in mid-summer contrasting in winter with trees covered in sparkling hoar frost.

There are changes among the birds, too, with the arrival and departure of thousands of migratory ducks, geese and swans throughout the year. In spring, birds take part in courtship rituals, showing off their magnificent plumage. From late spring until mid-summer, hatching is in full swing at most of the centres with delightful fluffy ducklings, goslings and cygnets all over the grounds. All but two of the centres have collections of wildfowl from around the world, including rare species for which special conservation measures are being taken.

WWT centres provide excellent facilities for visitors of all ages and abilities. These include birdwatching from well-designed hides and observatories, areas for quiet contemplation, shops and restaurants, events programmes of walks, talks and school holiday activities, exhibits and interpretation of waterbird and wetland issues, and learning programmes for schools and universities. WWT works with around 75,000 schoolchildren a year and develops a wide range of materials and activities related to the National Curriculum.

At **WWT Slimbridge**, large flocks of wild birds, including thousands of White-fronted Geese, several hundred Bewick's Swans and many different species of duck, return every winter to the protection and security of the reserve. Over 300 hectares of fields and saltmarsh are managed specifically for waterbirds. An extensive system of hides allows visitors to watch the birds without disturbing them. Visitors can also walk among one of the most diverse collections of wildfowl in the world, including all six species of flamingo. Crowning the visitor centre is the 17-metre Sloane Observation Tower (served by a lift), giving panoramic views of the reserve and the surrounding Severn Vale.

A beautiful wooded hillside and large castle form a magnificent backdrop to **WWT Arundel** in West Sussex. Landscaped lakes and meadows lie in a picturesque setting between the River Arun and Swanbourne Lake. Wildfowl, especially diving ducks, thrive in the fresh, clear spring waters. On the reserve, observation hides overlook wader scrapes and a splendid reedbed - designated an SSSI because of its importance to warblers. The new Wetland Discovery Area, opened in 2005, can be toured in silent electric boats which take wheelchairs.

The sound of a 25,000-strong dawn chorus of Barnacle Geese flying from their evening roost greets visitors to **WWT Caerlaverock** in autumn and winter, when this vital wetland area on the shores of the Solway Firth near Dumfries is home to the entire Svalbard population of Barnacle Geese. In the 1940s only 300 wintered on the Firth, but numbers have now increased astonishingly thanks to the protection they have been afforded. Caerlaverock also attracts thousands of Pink-footed Geese, Wigeon, Pintail, Teal and waders, and hundreds of Whooper Swans. Nesting Barn Owls can also be watched on a CCTV system. Other outstanding features are the new Granary Building and Saltcot Merse Observatory.

On the shores of Strangford Lough in County Down, just twelve miles from Belfast, **WWT Castle Espie** provides wonderful views of over 20,000 Light-bellied Brent Geese each autumn - virtually the entire population that migrates between Arctic Canada and Ireland - as well as huge flocks of ducks and waders. The centre is home to a delightful collection of wildfowl, and features a wildlife art gallery, and sustainable garden with pioneering water filtration system. It also hosts some of Ireland's major annual environmental events.

WWT London Wetland Centre in Barnes, opened in 2000, is the world's first purpose-built wetland reserve in a capital city. On the site of the former Barn Elms Reservoirs, 43 hectares of diverse wetland habitat - lagoons, reedbeds and grazing marsh - have been created from scratch, just six kilometres from Hyde Park Corner. In its first five years the London Wetland Centre has attracted 278 species of birds - including breeding Redshanks, Lapwings, Little Ringed Plovers and Pochard, and regular wintering Bitterns - and nearly a million human visitors. The centre won the British Airways Tourism for Tomorrow Global Award in 2001. There is a three-storey hide with a lift, while the main visitor building gives panoramic views across the reserve, and its restaurant is in itself an attraction to local people.

WWT Martin Mere, near Ormskirk, Lancashire, is one of the most important wintering sites in the UK for Pink-footed Geese - over 25,000 return every year from their Icelandic breeding grounds, joining over 1,800 Whooper Swans and thousands of ducks. Where once the largest lake in England existed, but was almost completely drained in the 17th century, WWT created a marshland reserve, and Martin Mere became the first WWT centre to be designated a Ramsar site in 1985. A 63 hectare extension of the reserve converted to wetlands in 2004 has quickly become important habitat for breeding waders and is overlooked by the spectacular Harrier Hide.

Set in a traditional industrial area of South Wales, **WWT National Wetlands Centre Wales,** near Llanelli, is an example of conservation and industry working together. Located on the internationally important Burry Inlet, the reserve attracts a great diversity of waterbirds, including, on the new Milennium Wetlands, a roost of several hundred Little Egrets in late summer and autumn: one of the largest in the UK. The centre is also home to a large collection of wildfowl including a flock of colourful Caribbean Flamingos.

WWT Washington, near Sunderland, is set in a shallow valley sloping down to the River Wear. Visitors can get close to hundreds of birds, including the rare Hawaiian Goose or Nene. Wild birds, especially Redshanks, use the lakes and pools as 'stopovers' during annual migration, and can be observed from hides, while there is a particularly interesting wild bird feeding station. The centre has a wild Heronry, and visitors can view these birds at extremely close quarters via a special closed circuit television system. At the Waterfowl Nursery newly hatched birds can be seen taking their first steps.

WWT Welney, on the Ouse Washes in Norfolk, is the most important site in Europe for wintering Bewick's and Whooper Swans. Pair bonding rituals, preening, feeding and the occasional squabble take place just a few feet from visitors sitting in comfort in the centrally-heated observatory. In winter, the centre also welcomes thousands of Pochard, Wigeon, Pintail, Teal, Gadwall and Shoveler, while summer residents include Garganey and Avocets. A major new visitor centre building is under construction and is due to open early in 2006, interpreting the remarkable Fenland heritage and providing direct access into the observatory for all visitors.

The centres are imporant for a wide range of wildlife other than wildfowl. For instance, Caerlaverock is the most northerly location for the globally threatened Natterjack Toad, while many of the centres have scarce wetland flora. A programme is under way to reintroduce a number of species of rare plants to Martin Mere.

WWT's Wider Work

For conservation programmes to be effective, information is continually needed about migration patterns, fluctuations in populations and changes in habitat, as well as basic waterbird behaviour and ecology. The experience gained over the last sixty years - both at the centres and elsewhere - and the quality of the scientific data collected is such that help and practical advice is sought and given to both governmental and non-governmental organisations all over the world. WWT gathers information about waterbirds and wetlands; develops techniques for creating, restoring, managing and increasing awareness of wetland habitats; and plans for the conservation of threatened species. Expert consultancy services in all these fields are provided through WWT's Wetlands Advisory Service (WAS).

WWT's Wetland Link International (WLI) programme, with contacts in more than 100 countries, seeks to increase effective contact between the growing number of wetland education/conservation centres around the world. Topics covered include educational programmes, training courses and designs for new centres. WLI produces a biannual newsletter for its participants and helps them to locate relevant expertise and exchange ideas. WWT is also leading efforts to develop a global wetland learning programme, in partnership with the Ramsar Convention and Wetlands International. In the UK, WWT is taking a lead in developing education and public awareness programmes in support biodiversity.

How You Can Help

The Wildfowl & Wetlands Trust is a registered charity which needs your help to continue its conservation work. For further details on how you can help, perhaps by becoming a member, and information about its programmes and centres visit www.wwt.org.uk, write to WWT, Slimbridge, Gloucester, GL2 7BT or telephone 0870 334400. The addresses and telephone numbers of WWT's other centres are:

WWT Arundel
Mill Road, Arundel, West Sussex, BN18 9PB (0870 334 4002)

WWT Caerlaverock
Eastpark Farm, Caerlaverock, Dumfriesshire, DG1 4RS (0870 334 4003)

WWT Castle Espie
78 Ballydrain Road, Comber, Co Down, BT23 6EA (0870 334 4004)

WWT London Wetland Centre
Queen Elizabeth's Walk, London, SW13 9WT (0870 334 4001)

WWT Martin Mere
Burscough, Ormskirk, Lancashire, L40 0TA (0870 334 4006)

WWT National Wetlands Centre Wales
Penclacwydd, Llwynhendy, Llanelli, Carmarthenshire, SA14 9SH
(0870 334 4005)

WWT Washington
Pattinson, Washington, Tyne & Wear, NE38 8LE (0870 334 4007)

WWT Welney
Hundred Foot Bank, Welney, Nr Wisbech, Cambridgeshire, PE14 9TN
(0870 334 4008)